A C User's Guide to ANSI C

Pradeepa Siva
PRODUCT INFORMATION COORDINATOR
CORPORATE & PROFESSIONAL PUBLISHING GROUP

Addison-Wesley Publishing Company
ONE JACOB WAY
READING, MASSACHUSETTS 01867
(617) 944-3700 EXT. 2940 FAX (617) 944-7273
70550.2022 COMPUSERVE
70550.2022@compuserve.com

Addison-Wesley Professional Computing Series

Brian W. Kernighan, Consulting Editor

Arnold/Peyton, *A C User's Guide to ANSI C*

Cargill, *C++ Programming Style*

Curry, *UNIX Systems Security: A Guide for Users and System Administrators*

Meyers, *Effective C++ 50 Specific Ways to Improve Your Programs and Designs*

Perlman, *Interconnections: Bridges and Routers*

Stevens, *Advanced Programming in the UNIX Environment*

A C User's Guide to ANSI C

Ken Arnold and John Peyton

ADDISON-WESLEY PUBLISHING COMPANY, INC.

Reading, Massachusetts Menlo Park, California New York
Don Mills, Ontario Wokingham, England Amsterdam
Bonn Paris Milan Madrid Sydney Singapore
Tokyo Seoul Taipei Mexico City San Juan

The publisher offers discounts on this book when ordered in quanity for special sales.
For more information please contact:

Corporate & Professional Publishing Group
Addison-Wesley Publishing Company
One Jacob Way
Reading, Massachusetts 01867

Cover design by Joyce Weston

ISBN 0-201-56331-2
1 2 3 4 5 6 7 8 9 10 MW 9594939291
First printing, January 1992

Contents

Preface

This book is designed to help current C users become proficient in ANSI C quickly. Rather than describe ANSI C completely, and expect the reader to notice what's new, we present a list of changes from the common dialects of C (K&R, BSD 4.3, System V.3, and a scattering of others) that a user of ANSI C should know about.

ANSI has changes ranging from the critical to the truly nitpicky. There are two kinds of critical changes. The most important are "quiet changes". These are changes in behavior without a change in syntax; in other words, existing code might act differently than it did under existing implementations, but the compiler can't warn you about it. Of course, some quiet changes are also unlikely to bite you, but the fact that you won't get warned by your compiler about the change in behavior makes it necessary to tell you about them anyway. The other critical changes are changes in syntax, which might require you to change your code to compile it under ANSI C.

We have split the book into two main sections, one for the language itself (including the preprocessor) and one for the library routines that provide run-time support. The language section is organized by category: tokens, the preprocessor, declarations, expressions, statements, and future directions. The library section is ordered by header file from most to least basic.

If you want to get a jump-start on ANSI C, you can scan the book for only the critical changes, which are marked by bars in the margin. However, it's a good idea to come back later and read the whole book, or you'll get bitten by something rarer or more subtle.

We also describe some techniques for making your code compile with both pre-ANSI and ANSI compilers. Until every system in the world is ANSI compliant, many programs will have to compile on both kinds of systems. These tricks are interspersed in the text where they are relevant.

Rather than merely recite changes, we have made an effort to describe unobvious reasons for them. This is for more than historical interest; we think it will be easier to remember *what* has changed if you know *why* it was changed. It can also sometimes help eliminate frustration by letting you know that the ANSI committee sometimes had no real choice, for reasons that may not be obvious. You will be annoyed and even angered by their decisions often enough; we thought to reduce this annoyance by giving you the excuses, although you — or even we — might not think them sufficient.

Although we are trying to present the material in a small space, we have not always been able to prevent our opinions on changes from creeping in. We do not view this book as a commentary on ANSI C, rather as an explication of it. However, our writing style is more conversational than that of many technical tomes, and sometimes we could not simply describe a particular travesty without making it clear that we did not approve. Otherwise we could never look at our reflections in the monitor again.

The book is written in the first person because only one of us was writing text at any given time. As regular readers of the *C Advisor* column in *UNIX Review* may note, the writing style is strongly Ken's. We hope you will read it anyway.

Primarily we have designed this book to be useful, rather than precise to the point of numbness; we are not reprinting the ANSI standard. We hope it is readable as a book, concise as a reference, and soon obsolete as you put this transition behind you and get on to *doing* things with the language instead of worrying about it. We suspect it might also make a pretty good flyswatter.

We would like to thank Steve C. Dewhurst, Patricia Giencke, Brian W. Kernighan, Douglas B. Robinson, and Clovis L. Tondo, for their diligent, helpful, and very insistent reviews. What errors remain in this book after their thorough work are hopefully insignificant, and are, in any case, completely our fault. We would also like to acknowledge Walter Murray's helpful discussions about some arcane edges of the standard. John Wait and the crew at Addison-Wesley suffered these novice authors with amazing forbearance and provided critical help and equipment. CPU cycles were supplied, in large part, by Kee Hinkley and his Amazing In-Home Computer Center.

This book would also not have been possible without the support of our families. Ken's wife, Susan D. Jones, and her mother Jill S. Jones, shouldered Ken's share of parenthood at long and odd intervals so that he could be an author when he probably ought to have been being a father. For that, and for monopolizing the home computer, he asks Jareth and Corwin's understanding (with a small bribe in the college fund department). John thanks his wife Judy for her faith and for yielding precious weekend time; also his father for his love of the mind.

Ken Arnold
John Peyton
13 October, 1991

Chapter 1 Introduction

ANSI C was designed to create a standard, portable C dialect. It took six years to come up with, and it is mind-numbingly precise. It leads many computer language experts to drone on in truly Talmudic debates about obscure boundary conditions, and, in general, the ANSI C standard is a crashing bore.

Given this, sane, sentient beings should ask themselves "Why should I care about ANSI C?" There are several reasons.

Pragmatism
: ANSI C is destined to become the common C base across almost all platforms. If you want to continue to write C, you'd better understand it. Also, more and more software libraries will be written in ANSI C, so if you want to keep up with new software tools, or the latest versions of the ones you already have, ANSI C will be foisted on you.

Improvements
: ANSI C has added some very useful mechanisms, both to the language and to the library. When you know how to use it, ANSI C will make your programming time more effective.

Paranoia
: If you don't understand the "quiet changes" to ANSI C, your existing code might break, and you would be left hunting around for your bug like a linebacker after a contact lens in the middle of a play. And, while you're hunting, somebody with cleats is bound to step on you.

1.1 How to Use This Book

This book is designed to help current C users learn ANSI C by describing the changes, rather than having them read a description of ANSI C and figure out what has changed.

To this end, it is designed to be two books, which can be read sequentially or concurrently. The first is an overview of the major changes that are most likely to make your program perform differently or not compile. The second is a more complete list of changes, including some rather abstruse or outlying tweaks to the language.

Of course, you are holding only one book right now, so I had to come up with a way to put these two books into one volume. I have marked the most critical changes with a bar on the outer margin (as you can see at the edge of this paragraph). It is quite possible to get a quick feel for the important changes by reading only sections marked with this bar and saving other sections for later reading. Or you can read the whole book, getting everything at once. The choice is yours.

I have marked four kinds of changes: "quiet changes", that might make existing code act differently; changes in syntax, which might require you to change your code to compile it under ANSI C; important portability issues; and major new functionality.

1.2 Who Is ANSI, Anyway?

The American National Standards Institute, commonly known as ANSI, is an independent standards-setting body. It produces standards on almost anything anybody could possibly care about, including nail sizes, condoms, and floor waxes. Not surprisingly, as use of software has become more widespread, programmers have become more interested in having standard, predictable software foundations on which to build their products. ANSI has undertaken standardization in many areas of software, including operating system interfaces, network protocols, and security.

ANSI has been concerned with computer languages for quite some time. ANSI has produced several FORTRAN and COBOL standards over the years. As C became a more popular programming language, the people who used it became more and more frustrated by the diverging implementations of both the language and the library routines that normally accompany it. This led to a desire to have a standard for the C language. So ANSI did what it always does: it formed a committee with membership open to all interested parties (for a fee). The majority of those who joined were from companies that made compilers, but there were also software development companies and some interested individuals who participated. This committee set out to come to some agreement on what standard C would be.

1.3 What ANSI Was Trying to Do

It will be helpful to know what the ANSI committee was trying to accomplish. They started with a language that was popular, but that had no formal specification. The de facto standard was *The C Programming Language* by Brian W. Kernighan and Dennis M. Ritchie (commonly called K&R), but this was somewhat out of date (it did not have `enum`, for example) and was subject to varying interpretations. When it was published, the C compiler shipped by AT&T (the Portable C Compiler, with the Reiser C preprocessor) differed from K&R, and as C was reimplemented on various platforms, it took on new features and changes in behavior. The X3J11 Technical Committee on the C Programming Language (the formal name for the ANSI C committee) was set up to rectify the problems of this divergence. However, ANSI was not, if possible, to define new mechanisms. They were to codify existing practice.

They defined for themselves the following guiding principles:

Existing code is important; existing implementations are not.
: The idea was, if possible, to avoid breaking most existing C code. On the other hand, no existing compilers were to be held up as a reference. Everyone was going to have to change, at least somewhat, to meet the ANSI standard.

C code can be portable.
: The standard was designed to work on as many platforms as it could without emasculating the language or library.

C code can be nonportable.
: The committee made no attempt to make it impossible, or even hard, to write non-portable code. The ability to write device drivers or locally tuned applications was considered a feature of the language to be preserved, not a bug to be squashed.

Avoid quiet changes.
: ANSI tried to avoid making changes to the meanings of existing C mechanisms that would, without warning, change a program's behavior when it was compiled under an ANSI compiler. This was not always possible; see Appendix A for a summary of the quiet changes.

A standard is a treaty between implementor and programmer.
: The standard defines many so-called *minimum maximums*, which are lower limits on the upper limits an implementation can provide. For example, no implementation may have a maximum local identifier length of fewer than 31 characters. This allows the programmer to rely on a certain set of minimum standards, without constraining a vendor from providing a higher limit as a value-added feature (although programs use such features at the risk of reduced portability).

Keep the spirit of C.
: The original C was designed as a programmer's language, one that trusted programmers to know what they were doing. Of course, as a current C user, you must know that this means that you can get yourself into weirder trouble faster in C than in almost any other language in widespread use. However, it also means that you can do exactly what you want without a Big Brother language telling you that it isn't "nice".

: C is also small and elegant, not overloaded with features or multiple ways to do things. It trusts to library packages for most extensions, including I/O (which is an integral part of most languages).

Overall, the ANSI committee kept pretty well to these constraints. There are some baffling violations, though, which I won't be able to resist pointing out when I describe them. And sometimes hewing to their goals made them lose sight of some more important strictures of language design (most notably in the syntax of function prototypes, where "existing practice" took precedence over "simple and elegant" in a most distressing way). Nonetheless, ANSI C provides an important tool for C portability. Besides, whether you like it or not (and I mostly do like it), if you program in C you will need to adapt to it, since it surely will become the dominant dialect of C.

1.4 Definition of Terms

I've adopted several terms that ANSI uses, and have also added some of my own. Here are definitions of the most common ones:

as if
: ANSI defines an abstract machine on which operations are defined. An implementation is allowed to implement things in any way it wants, as long as it does so *as if* the abstract machine definition were followed. This concept of doing things *as if* is fundamental to the standard.

compiler
: I use the word *compiler* throughout this book, although the ANSI standard is specifically designed to work with both compilers and interpreters. So when I say "compiler" I actually mean any C language processor.

conforming implementation
: An implementation of C (a compiler or interpreter) is *conforming* if it can compile any strictly conforming program (see below).

implementation defined behavior
: When behavior in certain circumstances is *implementation defined*, implementors may do what they wish, but they must document their choice.

implementor
: An *implementor* refers to someone who writes compilers and the standard libraries.

K&R
: *The C Programming Language* by Brian W. Kernighan and Dennis M. Ritchie, first edition. This was the closest thing there was to a written standard prior to ANSI.

maximally portable
: A strictly conforming program (see below) is *maximally portable*, since the result of making a program strictly conforming is a maximum degree of portability.

strictly conforming program
: A program is considered *strictly conforming* if it violates no rule of the standard, relies on no undefined, unspecified, or implementation defined behavior, and does not exceed any of the minimum maximums.

undefined behavior

When a program's behavior in certain circumstances is *undefined*, this means that when the programmer makes certain errors, implementors can do what they wish including drastic, dramatic, and completely incoherent behavior. Undefined behavior is usually allowed for error conditions that are difficult to detect, such as a mismatch between a function declaration in one file and the definition in another.

unspecified behavior

When a program's behavior in certain circumstances is *unspecified*, the implementor must translate the program, but some details are left to their discretion. Correct programs may rely on unspecified behavior. Examples of unspecified behavior are the order of evaluation of parameters to functions or whether strings are stored in read-only memory. Programs that rely on a compiler's specific implementation of such things are not strictly conforming.

The distinction between *undefined* and *unspecified* behavior is hard for everyone to keep straight. Simply put, it is a distinction between whether implementors need not catch an error that may cause horrific failure (undefined behavior) and whether implementors have some minor leeway in what they do with legal code where the standard is not explicit (unspecified behavior). Initializing a global variable in two files causes *undefined* behavior; the representation of floating-point numbers is *unspecified*.

Language

Chapter 2 Language

ANSI C leaves most of the C language intact. In many places what the standard provides is more detail in how various parts of the language, especially the preprocessor, work. There are some new features added, such as function prototypes and string concatenation and a few long-deprecated mechanisms removed. We have devoted a chapter to each major area of the language, and at the end of this section there is a chapter on future language directions.

2.1 Limits

There are several minimum maximums that ANSI guarantees for program translation. They are all listed in Appendix B; we only list some of the more important ones here:

- 8 nested **`#includes`**.
- 32 nested levels of parentheses in an expression. This might bite you on deeply nested macros, since macros are usually heavily parenthesized.
- 31 significant characters in an internal identifier or macro name. This isn't so bad until you see the next one.
- 6 significant characters in external identifiers, ignoring case. This is probably the ugliest limit, caused by constraints from existing loaders, but remember: many implementations will provide more than this. In fact, the committee stated that this limit is obsolescent, and they threaten to remove it forthwith, or as soon as they get around to it.
- 509 characters in a single logical source line. This means that long macros might run over.

- 509 characters in a character string literal (after concatenation). Watch out for long strings formed by concatenation.
- 127 members of a single `struct`, `union`, or `enum`. A large `enum` might hit this, but it's not likely.

Compilers may provide larger values for these limits; compiler implementors are also encouraged to let tables grow dynamically rather than having hard limits at all.

A compiler that imposes a limit on identifier length will usually let you type in more characters, but it just ignores them. For example, if you had a C compiler with an eight-character identifier limit, it would allow you to type in a local identifier with a longer name, such as `primblort`. However, since it doesn't use anything beyond the first eight characters, the compiler would accept any typo you made after those eight; for example, it would accept `primblorg` as equivalent to `primblort`. Under ANSI, these would be two separate identifiers, and, depending on their use, they might not generate a compiler error, but instead refer to two separate objects. This will break your code, and thus the increase in significant characters is a potential "quiet change".

Chapter 3 Tokens

3.1 What Is a Token?

The basic unit of compilation is the *token*, which is the smallest unit of recognizable meaning. It is analogous to a word in natural languages, in that it stands alone and can have meaning. In C, tokens are such things as operators, keywords, constants, and identifiers.

3.2 Keywords

The `entry` keyword, long reserved for future use in every C document, has been dropped.[1] So has `fortran`, which some compilers used to declare C-to-FORTRAN calls, and `asm`, which introduced raw assembly language instructions in many compilers.

Several new keywords have been added. They are `const`, `volatile`, `signed`, and (new for some) `void`. These will all be discussed in their appropriate places.

3.3 Constants

3.3.1 Suffix Modifiers

Several new kinds of constants have been added. Besides the suffix `l` (or alternately `L`) which denoted a `long` constant, ANSI has added `u` (or `U`) for unsigned constants (which can be used together with `l` or `L` as in `42ul`) and `f` (or `F`)which denotes a `float` (as

[1]When I say this, I always have this vision from those old movies where the jury returns to the courtroom, announces the verdict, and the reporters beat themselves silly to race for a phone and yell the result to their editor, only in my vision, they're yelling "`entry`'s gone, boss! `entry`'s gone!!!" Maybe I should see a psychiatrist.

opposed to a double) constant. A new use has been added for l and L; if either follows a floating-point constant, it denotes a long double constant (see Section 5.1 below).

3.3.2 Types of Integer Constants

In K&R, an integer constant too big for a signed int was taken to be a long. In ANSI it is unsigned int if that is big enough to hold its value. For example, on a machine with a 16-bit int, 0xffff would be a long with a value of -1 on many existing compilers, but under ANSI C it would be an unsigned int with a value of 65535. This means that hex and octal constants make lousy negative numbers.

People who try to define the most negative int will find themselves perplexed if they try (on a machine with a 16-bit int)

```
# define MIN_INT 0x8000
```

or even

```
# define MIN_INT -32768
```

Because both these constants are too large for an int, the compiler will treat them as unsigned int in any expression. You must provide an expression that yields that number, for example:

```
# define MIN_INT (-MAX_INT - 1)
```

3.3.3 Are String Constants Read-Only?

You cannot rely on strings being either read-only or *not* read-only, nor on having identical string constants being stored only once in memory, or stored separately. The standard says that all this is undefined. Code that uses a routine that modifies the string it is passed, such as:

```
char *tmpfile;

tmpfile = mktemp("/tmp/PrgXXXXXX");
```

or that uses a pointer to a string that may be conditionally modified:

```
char *sp = "keyword";

if (all_upper_case)
        upperize(sp);
```

is not guaranteed to work on ANSI compilers. You have the disadvantages of both read-only and writable strings, and none of the advantages of either.

3.3.4 Wide Character and String Constants

In order to accommodate written human languages with more characters than will fit in a byte, most notably many Asian languages, ANSI has added the concept of a wide character. Wide character strings or character constants are *preceded* by an `l` (or `L`). How the bits in such constants are interpreted is implementation defined, but the syntax is portable. Wide characters are of type `wchar_t`, which is defined in the header file `<stddef.h>` (see Chapter 10), and look like this:

```
L'\xE59'
```

Wide strings are arrays of `wchar_t` and look like this:

```
L"\xE59\x7F3 is long"
```

3.3.5 Reserved Names

ANSI has reserved to implementors most identifiers beginning with an underscore (_), as well as those defined in the standard library (see Chapter 24). If a programmer avoids these names, a conforming implementation should not conflict with any of the programmer's own identifiers.

3.4 String Concatenation

Adjacent string constants with no operators between them are simply concatenated. Quite simply, this means that the expression

```
"bo" "zo"
```

is exactly equivalent to

```
"bozo"
```

This is useful not only for macros (as we shall see) but also for long strings such as help messages. For example, we could have a help string such as

```
char *usage = "usage: quibble [-i] [-l lang] fact ...\n"
              "     -i:    quibble intensely\n"
              "     -l:    alternate language to quibble in\n";
```

and have a single, long, printable usage string (however, be careful of string length limits; see Section 2.1 above).

3.5 Escape Sequences

ANSI has added three more escape sequences: `\a` for "alert", which should ring a bell (control-G on most ASCII systems); `\v` for a vertical tab; and `\x` to introduce a hex constant, much as a \ followed by a digit introduces an octal constant.

ANSI has limited the number of digits in an octal character to a maximum of three (some non-ANSI compilers gobble up all they can). This means that `"\0334"` will not be some implementation defined form of octal 0334, but will be the character '\033' (which is the ASCII escape character) followed by the character '4'.

The hex form for escape would be \x1b. Unlike the octal form, the hex number is taken to be the longest string it can be; for example, "\x1bC" does not generate the sequence "<ESCAPE>C", but whatever character the compiler would assign to the hex value 1BC.[2] If you needed to put "<ESCAPE>C", in a string, you would use string concatenation like this:

```
"\x1b" "C"
```

A strange side effect of the fact that octal escape sequences have at most three characters is that some but not all wide characters can be expressed in octal. Any wide character above 0777 must be written in hex. Weird, but true.

The digits 8 and 9 are no longer allowed as part of octal constants. This may seem bizarre to point out ("You mean they ever were?"), but many compilers would accept "\128" as equivalent to "\130". The only problem is that our first character constant has a different meaning now in ANSI; the rule that says to gobble up all possible digits now stops sooner, and "\128" now yields a two-character string of \12 followed by the ASCII digit 8.

Implementors are free to do what they want with an undefined escape sequence, and ANSI has decided to reserve all sequences of \ followed by a lowercase letter for future escape sequences. You should avoid undefined escape sequences (that is, \ followed by a lowercase letter) if you want to keep your code portable to other machines or compatible with future versions of ANSI C.

3.6 Trigraphs

There are several characters necessary for C programming that don't necessarily exist in non-ASCII character sets. For the use of the poor souls working in such character sets, ANSI added trigraphs to the language as substitutes for these characters. It should be noted that trigraphs have their meaning both inside and outside strings and characters. I hope none of you ever has to use them, but you should know what they are, so see the table below. Anything that starts with ?? but is not a trigraph is left intact.

To defend the reputation of the ANSI committee, let me quote from their rationale on this point: "The Committee makes no claims that a program written using trigraphs looks attractive." To prove their point, let us look at a small, useless example without trigraphs and then with:

```
#define IS_GOODIE       0x8

if (flagset & IS_GOODIE) {
        flagset &= ~IS_GOODIE;
        toggles[i] ^= was_goodie;
        cleared[i] |= TRUE;
        printf("Added a Goodie!\n");
}
```

[2] As always, what is done with values outside the legal range for a char is implementation defined.

Trigraph	*Becomes*
`??=`	`#`
`??'`	`^`
`??!`	`|`
`??/`	`\`
`??-`	`~`
`??(`	`[`
`??)`	`]`
`??<`	`{`
`??>`	`}`

Figure 3.1: Trigraphs

```
??=define        IS_GOODIE        0x8

if (flagset & IS_GOODIE) ??<
        flagset &= ??-IS_GOODIE;
        toggles??(i??) ??'= was_goodie;
        cleared??(i??) ??!= TRUE;
        printf("Added a Goodie!??/n");
??>
```

Note that this makes the not-unimaginable string `"Really???!?!??!"` become `"Really?|?!|"`, so you've got to be a little careful.

Chapter 4 Preprocessor

C wouldn't be C without its preprocessor. The preprocessor is the part of C that processes those `#` directives. The macro language provided by the preprocessor is relatively limited, but quite useful and widely used. In ANSI, there are some new features and semantics, and two areas of major incompatible change.

4.1 #include

First, there is an extension to the `#include` syntax. Besides being able to say both

```
# include       <header.h>
# include       "header.h"
```

it is now possible to use a macro name for the file name, as in

```
# define        LOCAL_NAMES     <someplace/names.h>

# include       LOCAL_NAMES
```

This will be mostly useful in using `#if` to set up the macros for the file names, rather than using `#if` around the actual includes. Like several other ANSI C extensions, this really adds no new functionality, but changes the cosmetics. If you have a header that can live in one of two places, it is often better to use the new form so that the `#if` that chooses the files to include is independent of the actual inclusion. Otherwise you will have two (or more) `#include` lists, which will have to be maintained in parallel, and we all know how often that kind of thing breaks down.

It should be noted that you cannot use string concatenation to build `#include` header file names, since they are not string constants. You can, however, use `##` concatenation (see Section 4.2.2 below).

4.2 #define

There have also been some changes that allow interesting use of macro names. For example, if you want all your `fopen()` calls to use the new `b` modifier (see Section 11.2 below), you could redefine `fopen()` in terms of itself without fear of infinite expansion:

```
/* use string concatenation to add "b" to all fopen() modes */
# define        fopen(file,mode)        fopen(file, mode "b")
```

(I would generally recommend against this kind of usage, since it hides the changed semantics of `fopen()` in a macro potentially far away from its use.)

To allow this "recursion", a process is followed which is worth describing, if for no other reason than I get to use one of the more amusing technical terms introduced into the C lexicon: "painted blue". While a macro is being expanded, it is temporarily undefined, and any recurrence of the macro name is (I kid you not, this is the standard terminology) *painted blue* so that in any future scans of the text it will not be expanded recursively. (I do not know why the color blue was chosen; I'm sure it was the result of a long debate, spread over several meetings.) Before expansion in the macro text, macro parameters are expanded, and then their expansions are placed in the macro's expanded text. All this is again rescanned for expansion, marking further expansions with blue paint, until there are no more valid expansions. Then the blue paint is erased, and the resulting text is passed on to the next phase of compilation.

This mechanism will also allow you to use macro names as parameters to other macros. Why you would want to is more of a mystery — it just turns invocation of a macro into an indirect invocation of a macro, but I'm sure some pectorally endowed person named Mongo insisted that this was critical.

4.2.1 String Substitution

Up to now, I've been discussing things that are directly borrowed from existing implementations of C. Where the existing implementations differed, one form was chosen so that there would be no ambiguity about behavior. The general insistence on existing practice was a guiding rule of the ANSI C committee, since it gave some assurance that a feature worked in some potentially useful fashion. Even the blue paint is a formalism of existing preprocessor behavior. Where they felt they could, ANSI avoided inventing new mechanisms.

However, I must present some sad historical background that led ANSI to decide that it had to invent new preprocessor syntax. The version of the preprocessor most commonly used on UNIX is called the Reiser preprocessor, after its author, John Reiser. Several vendors, however, chose to implement their own preprocessors.

Due to differences in interpretation of the C bible of the time (namely, K&R), two areas of divergence crept in, one on embedding macro parameters in strings, and the other on concatenation of macro parameters into single identifiers. The difference amounted to this — in Reiser it was possible to do these things, and in some other preprocessors one or both were impossible.

You would think that ANSI could have just picked the existing Reiser syntax, but, alas, the two existing practices were incompatible. Take, for example,

```
# define        PR_INT(val)      printf("val = %d\n", val)

PR_INT(i);
```

In Reiser, this would be expanded to

```
printf("i = %d\n", i);
```

but in other preprocessors, it would be

```
printf("val = %d\n", i);
```

If ANSI had chosen Reiser's mechanism, unexpected things would happen to people expecting non-Reiser-like behavior. Furthermore, there was strong feeling that Reiser's mechanism of scanning inside strings and character constants for parameter replacement was just plain ugly. They argued that the inconsistent definition of a token was confusing, as well as being hard to implement in compilers where the preprocessor was not a separate program but was built into the C language scanner itself.

So they chose the non-Reiser behavior (don't replace parameters inside strings) and invented new syntax for string values of parameters. (Please excuse me for a moment while I regain my calm and avoid describing my opinion of this decision. Thank you.) The new mechanism for insertion of parameters into strings relies on another new feature of ANSI C: string concatenation. ANSI has added a "string version of parameter" operator to the preprocessor, namely

#*param*

Using this together with string concatenation we would rewrite our `PR_INT()` example as:

```
# define        PR_INT(val)      printf(#val " = %d\n", val)
```

The `#val` would expand to a quoted version of (say) `"i"`, which would then be concatenated with the rest of the format string.

I must point out that in Reiser it was possible to create character constants using macro parameter names. For example,

```
# define        CTRL(x) ('x' & 0x1f)
```

would allow you to say `CTRL(S)` or `CTRL(Q)`. There is no way to rewrite this macro in ANSI; its invocation must be changed. The closest you can get is

```
# define        CTRL(x) (x & 0x1f)
```

allowing you to say `CTRL('S')` or `CTRL('Q')`. This lack is very unfortunate, because it makes adapting to the change a larger open-ended problem (fix all the invocations of such a macro in all source files) than it had to be (fix the **#define** of such a macro in its header file).

Right about now about a third of you more clever types have decided that I must have wet rubber rocks in my head. You think you've found a way to write my `CTRL()` macro, namely something like this:

```
# define        CTRL(x) (#x[0] & 037)
```

Thus

```
CTRL(L)
```

becomes

```
("L"[0] & 037)
```

For each of you who noticed this work-around, let me just tell you to wipe that smug look off your face. String constants are arrays of **char**, and ANSI does not allow array operators in constant expressions (although it probably could have). Thus, `"L"[0]` cannot be a constant expression, and so (here's the punch line) cannot be used as a value for a **case** label. You could say:

```
if (ch == CTRL(L))
        refresh();
else if (ch == CTRL(H))
        erase();
```

but not

```
switch (ch) {
  case CTRL(L):
        refresh();
        break;
  case CTRL(H):
        erase();
        break;
}
```

4.2.2 Parameter Concatenation

The second new mechanism is the concatenation operator `##` which allows you to create a whole new token out of two components.

For example, you might want to trigger a set of function invocations off a passed-in key:

```
# define STORE(type,v)  do {                          \
                            if (!known_## type(v))  \
                                add_ ## type(v);    \
                        } while (0)
```

Then, if you had the functions `known_name()`, `add_name()`, `known_child_no()`, and `add_child_no()` you could invoke the macro as either

```
STORE(name, "Corwin");
```

or

```
STORE(child_no, 2);
```

Let us follow these through their expansion sequences without the pro forma `do` loop (explained below):

```
STORE(name, "Corwin");
        ↓
if (!known_ ## name("Corwin")) add_ ## name("Corwin");
        ↓
if (!known_name("Corwin")) add_name("Corwin");

STORE(child_no, 2);
        ↓
if (!known_ ## child_no(2)) add_ ## child_no(2);
        ↓
if (!known_child_no(2)) add_child_no(2);
```

As you can see, to add a new type to this mechanism, you would just have to write the "known" and "add" functions, and provide the new type's name to any invocation of the `STORE()` macro. It is perfectly legal to have spaces around the `##` if you like.

Some of you may be wondering why I used the `do` loop when defining `STORE()`. This is a trick, predating ANSI, that allows a macro requiring more than one statement to be used anywhere a statement is legal. If `STORE()` was defined simply with the `if`, or inside the curly braces but without the `do while`, it would give surprising or illegal results in the following code:

```
if (add_name)
        STORE(name, "Jareth");
else
        STORE(child_no, 1);
```

In the if-only case, the else would be attached to the hidden if in the STORE() macro. In the curly-brace-only case, the else would be illegal, since it would be preceded by a close curly brace from the macro and the semicolon after the invocation of STORE(). If you want multistatement macros that are usable in every expected place, you need to enclose them in the do construct above, or in an if else construct, like this:

```
# define STORE(type,v)  if (1) {                       \
                               if (!known_ ## type(v)) \
                                   add_ ## type(v);    \
                            } else
```

I prefer the do form, since the if else form has surprising results should the programmer forget to add the semicolon after the invocation, making any following statement part of the macro's hidden else. With the do form, such a mistake would result in illegal syntax, so the compiler would generate an error.

4.3 #undef

The #undef directive is ignored if the symbol being undefined is not, in fact, currently defined. This means that compilers that currently protest about such directives should shut up.

4.4 defined()

ANSI has codified the defined() preprocessor built-in, which expands to 1 if the given symbol is defined, or 0 if it is not. In other words,

```
#if defined(__STDC__) || defined(c_plusplus) || \
        defined(__cplusplus)
# define        _PROTOTYPES
#endif
```

will define _PROTOTYPES in the same cases as

```
#ifdef __STDC__
# define        _PROTOTYPES
#endif
#ifdef c_plusplus
# define        _PROTOTYPES
#endif
#ifdef __cplusplus
# define        _PROTOTYPES
#endif
```

and is a lot prettier (and more modular) to boot.

4.5 #elif

The new **#elif** directive is, not surprisingly, an "else if". The preprocessor has needed one for a long time, although why "elif" instead of "elseif" or even "else if" is beyond me. Maybe they decided that a fuller form would be too much typing for the spirit of C.

There is no **#elifdef** or **#elifndef**. If you need these, you can use **#elif** with the **defined()** built-in.

4.6 #error

The new control

#error *text*

will generate a compile-time diagnostic with the given text. This is useful if you have an error the preprocessor can detect, such as a macro's not having one of the proper values:

```
#if SYSTYPE == BSD
/* BSD stuff */
#elif SYSTYPE == SYSV
/* sysV stuff */
#else
#   error SYSTYPE must be either BSD or SYSV
#endif
```

Executing a **#error** also makes the preprocessor phase fail so the compilation will be recognized as unsuccessful. Obviously a **#warning** would have been useful, but it wasn't added. A way to print out the value of a macro in a **#error** would also have been useful; the example will print out the name **SYSTYPE**, not the value of the **SYSTYPE** macro.

4.7 #pragma

The ANSI committee was wise enough to give people a hook for local extensions (since otherwise implementors pollute the language with them). Every ANSI compiler will accept any line starting with

```
#pragma
```

If what follows after the **#pragma** makes sense to the compiler, the line will be processed; otherwise it will be ignored, although a diagnostic message might be generated. This allows mechanisms controlling such things as inline expansion of common routines (such as **strcmp()** and **printf()**), compression of structures in memory, and so on, to be inserted into code portably. I use the term "portably" with some trepidation here, since it is possible that, say,

```
#pragma INLINE
```

might turn on inline expansion in one system and turn it off in another — there is *no* standard for strings that follow **#pragma**. This is probably okay in the long run, since most compiler writers will attempt to avoid collisions, but I'm sure there will be some problems somewhere. In any case, **#pragma** is still quite useful in the real world.

4.8 Predefined Symbols

To the predefined preprocessor macros `__FILE__` (the current source file as a quoted string) and `__LINE__` (the current line number as an integer), ANSI has added `__DATE__` and `__TIME__` which give, respectively, the date and time as quoted strings.

These can be useful for compiled-in strings. For example, if you want to provide an option that prints out when the program was last built, you could have code such as:

```
switch (option) {
  case 'b':
        printf("Last built " __DATE__ ", " __TIME__ "\n");
        break;
        /* ... */
}
```

If you want to print out debug information, it is often useful to have the source code line number printed, too. You could have a debug statement that looked like this:

```
if (Debug)
        printf(__FILE__":"__LINE__": x = %d, y = %d\n", x, y);
```

ANSI has also added the variable `__STDC__`, which has a value of `1` in ANSI-conforming compilers. This is tricky: several existing compilers predefine `__STDC__` to indicate that they implement some parts of ANSI (function prototypes is the most common example). So

```
#ifdef __STDC__
```

is the correct test to see if your code is being compiled under ANSI, but it turns out not to be a guarantee; anyone is free to define this symbol for any reason. However, if your vendor ships you a compiler that turns on `__STDC__`, but is *not* full ANSI C, maybe you should hire Mongo (see Section 4.2 above) to go straighten them out.

4.9 White Space before

On the minor side, it is now legal for white space (spaces or tabs) to precede as well as follow the **#**. In many preprocessors the **#** had to be the first character on the line; in some, it couldn't be followed by white space either. Now it's a free-for-all. I still recommend putting the **#** first in most instances for clarity and tradition.

4.10 Stuff after #else and #endif

Many existing compilers would ignore anything on a line after a **#else** or **#endif**. Many people used this to indicate to which **#if** the construct was tied, as in

```
#ifndef SYSV
        bsd_compute();
#else SYSV
        sysv_compute();
#endif SYSV
```

This usage was rather hard to specify formally and seemed to imply that there might be some checking by the preprocessor to make sure that the trailing stuff somehow *did* match the corresponding **#if**.

To eliminate these problems, the committee eliminated the feature. If you want to put such a comment on your **#else** or **#endif**, you can use a real comment:

```
#ifndef SYSV
        bsd_compute();
#else /* SYSV */
        sysv_compute();
#endif /* SYSV */
```

Then it is clear to all concerned that these are merely comments, not some error-checking mechanism for the preprocessor. Luckily this should only take a simple script to fix in existing code.

Chapter 5 Declarations

5.1 New Types

ANSI has added one new type to C, `long double`, which is to a `double` what a `long` is to an `int`; it is guaranteed to be at least as precise as a `double`. It can be used when you need the highest available floating-point precision, although if you get more precision, you will almost always pay a price in space and time.

5.2 New Meanings for Old Types

5.2.1 void

For a few of you, the `void` type is new. It has three uses.

First, if you declare a function with a return type of `void`, it means that the function returns no value. For example, the prototype for `exit()` looks like this:

```
void    exit(
                int     status
        );
```

Second, a function with a prototype parameter specification of `void` denotes a function which takes no arguments. For example, the prototype for `getchar()` is

```
int     getchar(void);
```

(See Section 5.5.2 below for more details on function prototypes.)

Third, `void *` is now the "generic pointer". Prior to the introduction of `"void *"`, the generic pointer was, by convention, a `char *`. This is no longer true, thank goodness. Any pointer to any data type may be converted into a `void *` and back again. This "there and back again" behavior also applies to casts between one function pointer type and another, although there is no generic function pointer in ANSI C. Other casts are problematic and should be avoided.

Besides the added clarity, using `void *` instead of `char *` for a generic pointer can also help the compiler catch some simple errors you might make. For example, incrementing a `void *` is illegal, whereas incrementing a `char *` will get you to the next byte. If you aren't pointing at a `char`, this can get you to very illegal places.

5.2.2 enum

Existing compilers provide different levels of strictness when dealing with `enum` constants, ranging from completely strict (you could not even use them to subscript arrays) to none at all (making them equivalent to a series of `#define`d integers). ANSI chose something in the middle, where an `enum` constant is always usable as an `int`, but an `enum` variable is typed when operating with other `enum` variables. Thus, it is legal to use a member of an `enum` as an array subscript (for example, to get a printable version of its name), but not to assign an `enum` variable to a variable of a different `enum`. It is, however, legal to assign a constant of one `enum` to a variable of another, since (a) an `enum` constant is usable as an `int`, and (b) an `int` can be assigned to any `enum` variable. This is a little surprising, but you'll have to live with it. To help elucidate, here are examples of legal and illegal uses of `enum` variables and constants, with the illegal one marked:

```
enum color {
        red, green, blue
};

enum president {
        washington, nixon, ford
};

enum color      shade;
enum president  executive;

void
test_enum()
{
        int     tmp;

        shade = red;
        shade = nixon;          /* legal, but questionable */
        shade = (enum color) executive;
        tmp = executive;
        shade = tmp;
        shade = executive;      /* illegal */
}
```

A minor syntactic point: some current compilers accept an optional trailing comma after the last identifier in an `enum`, to be analogous with initialization lists. ANSI doesn't allow this, which is just more random breakage for no good gain.

Some compilers accept integral type declarations such as `long` or `unsigned short` as part of an `enum`. ANSI C does not allow this.

5.2.3 Sign of char

In addition to all the type specifiers you already know, ANSI has added `signed`, which is mostly an explicit way of stating the default inverse of `unsigned`. However, in the case of `char`, ANSI has left the default undefined, since systems vary widely on whether a `char` is signed or unsigned. The `signed` specifier allows you to be explicit if you are trying to use a `char` for a very small integer. Your strings should be made of simple `char`s, since all the library routines expect `char *`, not `unsigned char *` or `signed char *`.

5.2.4 Bitfields

Bitfields in structures are, like `char`, ambiguous as to signedness. If you want to rely on whether a bitfield is treated as `signed` or `unsigned`, you must be explicit.

While we're on the subject of bitfields, it should be noted that ANSI restricts the types allowed for bitfields to `int`, `unsigned int`, and `signed int`. Some existing compilers allow other integral types (such as `long` and `short`). Unfortunately, the elimination of `long` as a legal bitfield type means that the longest bitfield you can portably create is 16 bits, the minimum size of an `int`.

5.2.5 Pointers to Arrays

ANSI C has made pointers to arrays meaningful. Now if you take the address of an array, instead of getting a pointer to the first element of the array you get a pointer to the array itself. What this means is that you can actually have pointers to multidimensional arrays and have the compiler take care of the indexing for you. For example, consider the following:

```
int     iarray[XSIZE][YSIZE];
int     (*ap)[YSIZE];

ap = &iarray[0];

ap[x][y] = 0;
```

Since `ap` is a pointer to an array with a known size, the compiler can do subscript calculation on it in a way impossible with simple pointers to objects.

This is also useful when dynamically allocating multidimensional arrays, for which the only portable mechanisms prior to ANSI were having multiple levels of indirections or calculating array indices by hand. An `XSIZE` by `YSIZE` dynamically allocated array could be acquired like this:

```
ap = (int (*)[YSIZE]) malloc(XSIZE * sizeof *ap);
```

Also, since ap is really a pointer to an array, ap++ will move you to the next array, allowing you to step through an array of arrays. For example, you could loop through all the subarrays of iarray by saying:

```
for (ap = &iarray[0]; ap < &iarray[XSIZE]; ap++)
        print_array(*ap);
```

All in all, the standardization of array pointers is a distinct advantage of ANSI C.

Notice that to get this new type you must explicitly take the address of the array. The name of an array is still a pointer to its first element. Many existing compilers accept &array as an alias for array (and generate a warning). Such code is now illegal, since the types of the pointers will not match.

5.3 Old Types Going Away

The long float alias for double supported by some compilers is now illegal.

Some compilers allowed a typed enum, such as long enum or unsigned enum. ANSI does not allow this. Nor does it allow you to use typedefed types with type specifiers such as short or long. For example, the following is illegal:

```
typedef int     int_t;

short int_t     shint;
```

5.4 Type Qualifiers

ANSI has added two type qualifiers to C: const and volatile.

5.4.1 volatile

The volatile qualifier tells the compiler that the variable may change in ways the compiler cannot predict. In effect, it is a directive to the compiler not to optimize references to that variable. Otherwise the compiler may feel free to think that, say, since it just put 12 into a variable that the value of that variable is 12. If the variable is volatile, the compiler can't do this. This is mostly useful for setjmp() (see Chapter 20), but it is also useful for device registers and multithreaded code.

5.4.2 const

The const qualifier is more commonly useful. It says that the object of that type will not be modified (with the exception of some qualifications described below). This has two advantages: the compiler can refuse a request to change the value of the object (otherwise it isn't a const, is it?), and the compiler can do broader optimizations, knowing that the value will remain unchanged in some situations.

5.4.3 Usage

Figuring out how to use the `const` and `volatile` qualifiers to get the effect you want can be tricky. For example, the declaration

```
const char      *sp;
```

means that `sp` will only point at characters that will not be modified through `sp` (although they might be modified through some other pointer). It does not mean that `sp` cannot be modified. To declare that, you would say

```
char            *const sp;
```

And an unmodifiable pointer to an unmodifiable `char` would be

```
const char      *const sp;
```

The only way I can help you is to point out that this follows the standard C declaration practice of saying that the expression represented by the declaration yields the type specified. For example,

```
char            *sp
```

means that `*sp` yields a `char`. Similarly,

```
const char      *sp
```

says that `*sp` yields a `const char`. To read the declaration

```
const char      *const sp;
```

you might say that `sp` is a `const` that, when dereferenced, yields a `const char`. You might also say that this is arcane, but if you think about it for a while, either your brain will turn to mush (and there will be more jobs for the rest of us, assuming your current job requires people who don't have mush for brains) or you will see that there isn't really any clearer way to extend the original C declaration syntax. If you *do* see one, sorry. It's too late.

It should be noted that *initializing* a `const` object is different from *modifying* it. It is legal to say

```
const int       True = 1;
const int       False = 0;
```

This gives `True` and `False` initial values that cannot legally be modified. And, while we're looking at qualifications to the unmodifiability of `const` variables, I'd like to reemphasize that a pointer to a `const` (such as `const char *sp`) simply means that it won't be modified *through that pointer*. Another pointer to the same place that is not declared `const` may be used to modify the value.

Use of `const` and `volatile` with arrays is somewhat interesting. A declaration of

```
const int       iarray[10];
```

declares that `iarray` is an array of `const int`, not that `iarray` itself is `const`. There is no way in the standard to get a `const` array, although this is not a big problem since an array which is, itself, `const` without its elements being `const` is meaningless.

Functions can return `const` or `volatile` values, but it is undefined to declare a function to be `const` or `volatile`. You can make such a declaration through a `typedef`:

```
typedef int              ifunc(void);
typedef const ifunc      const_func;
```

Functions that are of type `const_func` will now be `const`. A compiler may choose to assign some meaning to this (for example, as an assertion that the function has no side effects), but different compilers may assign different meanings, so maximally portable code should not use this.

5.4.4 const versus #define and enum

There are three ways to declare constants in ANSI C; `#define`, `const`, and `enum`. `enum` is most useful as a shorthand for a sequentially increasing `#define`. It does have some type-checking characteristics when using `enum` variables with other `enum` variables, but the interchangeability of `enum` constants with `int` makes them almost indistinguishable from a set of `#define` integer constants.

A `const` variable cannot be part of a constant expression, so it cannot be used for array dimensions or `case` labels. The main advantage a `const` constant has over other constants is that it is type checked like any other variable, and can be of any type, including `struct`. You can also take its address, which you cannot do with a `#define` or `enum` constant. As an added benefit, most debuggers don't remember preprocessor symbols, but a `const` or `enum` identifier would be remembered, making debugging on these machines a little easier.

5.5 Functions

5.5.1 Function Prototypes

In addition to declaring the return type of a function, you can now declare the type of the function's parameters. Such a declaration is commonly called a *prototype* or *signature*. Prototypes allow the compiler to do type checking and to avoid unnecessary promoting of parameters when calling functions. This is a great idea, since many program errors in C are caused by passing the wrong number or types of parameters. Unfortunately, the ANSI committee made a grave error when it chose the syntax.

5.5.2 Prototype Syntax

Let us look at an example. The prototype for the `fopen()` call might look like this:

```
FILE    *fopen(
                const char      *path,
                const char      *mode
        );
```

The syntax was borrowed almost completely from C++, which is an object-oriented extension of C.[1] Now let us give you the major caveats:

(1) There are now two distinct syntaxes for declaring variables in C: the (new) one for function parameters, and the (old) one for everything else.

(2) Note that the parameter declarations are comma separated, instead of semicolon terminated, as other declarations are. This means that you must declare the type of each parameter separately, even if two consecutive ones are of the same type. The prototype

```
double  pow(
                double  x, y
        );
```

will not work, since only `x` is given a type.

(3) The last parameter to a prototype must have the comma left off. This is different from the list in an array or `struct` initialization, in which a trailing comma is optional. Why this is recognized as being useful in one place and not the other is beyond me.

If you conclude, after reading this, that this very useful advance in C could have had more thought devoted to the usability of its syntax, you win a cigar (although the Surgeon General won't let you smoke it).[2]

The variable names in the prototype are optional, but in most cases they add some documentation. For example, if you're always wondering which parameter of `fread()` is the element size and which is the count, the prototype

```
size_t  fread(void *, size_t, size_t, FILE *);
```

isn't much help, but

```
size_t  fread(
                void    *buf,
                size_t  element_size,
                size_t  num_elements,
                FILE    *stream
        );
```

might give you a clue.

A trailing `...` means that there can be zero or more parameters after this point. For example, the prototype for `fprintf()` might look like:

```
int     fprintf(
                FILE            *fp,
                const char      *fmt,
                ...
        );
```

[1] For more information on C++, read *The Annotated C++ Reference Manual*, Margaret A. Ellis and Bjarne Stroustrup, Addison-Wesley, 1990.

[2] For a list of possible alternatives, see Appendix D; I won't bore you with such wishful thinking here.

Arguments that appear in place of the `...` go through the same type-widening rules that old-style functions do; for example, `float` becomes `double`, and `char` and `short` become `int`.

I'm sure some people out there are jumping up and down saying, "But what about functions with no parameters?!??!" I invite the rest of you to hunt them down and tell them to get a life. It *is* an intelligent question, but I can't stand know-it-alls who ask questions I'm just about to answer anyway.

The problem is that the obvious syntax for a function with no parameters would be to declare no parameters in the prototype, for example,

```
int     getchar();
```

This conflicts with the old syntax, in which this declaration means the moral equivalent (in the new syntax) of

```
int     getchar(...);
```

that is, it takes zero or more arguments. (This syntax is actually illegal; functions with `...` must have at least one explicit parameter. Sigh.) The compiler would not be able to distinguish an old-style declaration from a new one, so the compiler couldn't warn you that you were passing an unexpected argument to `getchar()`. Therefore, there is a special case in the new syntax for a prototype of a no-argument function, which is:

```
int     getchar(void);
```

I've been using standard system routines as examples, since you know what their actual prototypes are. However, you should never declare prototypes for standard library routines. You should always get them from a standard system header file. Functions are generally declared in the header file associated with them. For example, all the standard I/O functions have prototypes in `<stdio.h>`. For the mass of functions that don't really have an associated header file, you are likely to find them in the new file `<stdlib.h>`. Appendix C has a list of which header file has each function, type, or macro.

General All-Purpose Hint to Save Your Life

Always, *always*, include the header file that declares a function prototype in the source file that implements the function, not just in source files that call it. If you don't, you will either shoot yourself in shame after searching for a bug caused by a discrepancy between the prototype and the code, or your fellow programmers will shoot you in anger when they find out that the bug they've been tracking was due to such a discrepancy. In either case, the gunshot will increase the discharge of chemicals harmful to the ozone and hasten the day when this planet is a barren, seared, lifeless ball of dust. So do the Earth a favor and heed this advice.

As you may have noticed, it is very common to use `const` in function prototypes. Many functions take pointers to data, such as strings or structures, which they do not modify. Telling the user and compiler this in the prototype is an all-round Nice Thing to Do:

```
int     strcmp(
                const char      *string1,
                const char      *string2
        );
```

This lets the compiler assume that the values of the strings haven't been changed by **strcmp()**, which is helpful, and lets users know that they don't have to worry when they give you pointers to their private parts.

5.5.3 Writing Header Files

Some other caveats on real-world portable use of prototypes are in order here. On many systems, whether a source file is compiled under ANSI C or pre-ANSI C is a user's choice. This means that if you are writing a header file for a library that others will use, you cannot tell whether your functions are going to be called by code compiled with prototypes or without them. This has two major consequences for library routines that are meant to be called from code other people write.

First, your header file needs to be compilable under both prototype and nonprototype systems. There are several ways to use the preprocessor to have one header file for both (which is highly preferable to maintaining two headers that must be kept in sync). Here's one way:

```
#if defined(__STDC__) || defined(c_plusplus) ||  \
        defined(__cplusplus)
# define        _PROTOTYPES
#endif

#ifdef __cplusplus
/* required for C++ 2.0, 2.1, ... */
extern "C" {
#endif

FILE    *fopen(
#ifdef _PROTOTYPES
                        const char      *path,
                        const char      *mode
#endif
                );

int     fprintf(
#ifdef _PROTOTYPES
                        FILE            *stream,
                        const char      *fmt,
                        ...
#endif
                );
```

```
#ifdef __cplusplus
}
#endif

#undef _PROTOTYPES
```

Okay, okay. I've snuck in some C++ stuff so that the header is compilable not only with ANSI and non-ANSI C, but also with C++ versions 1.2 and 2. That's why I don't just `#if` on `__STDC__`, but on `c_plusplus` (C++ 1.2) and `__cplusplus` (C++ 2.0 and beyond) as well. So sue me.[3]

Another mechanism would look like

```
#if defined(__STDC__) || defined(c_plusplus) ||  \
        defined(__cplusplus)
# define        _PROTOTYPE(func,args)   func args
#else
# define        _PROTOTYPE(func,args)   func()
#endif

#ifdef __cplusplus
/* required for C++ 2.0, 2.1, ... */
extern "C" {
#endif

_PROTOTYPE(FILE *fopen, (
                                const char      *path,
                                const char      *mode
                        ));
_PROTOTYPE(int fprintf, (
                                FILE            *stream,
                                const char      *fmt,
                                ...
                        ));

#ifdef __cplusplus
}
#endif

#undef _PROTOTYPE
```

Always put such a `#define` after the last `#include` of another header file, and do the `#undef` at the end, too, so you don't pollute the name spaces of other headers or your users' source.

[3] For your code to be fully C++ includable avoid C++'s added keywords like this: `class` and `private`. Reading any current C++ book is recommended if this matters to you. And if you're writing header files for libraries others will use, it should. The current full list of added C++ keywords (version 2.1) is `asm`, `catch`, `class`, `delete`, `friend`, `inline`, `new`, `operator`, `private`, `protected`, `public`, `template`, `this`, `throw`, `try`, and `virtual`. However, there is already an ANSI C++ committee at work, so ...

Another point is that with prototypes, many compilers optimize their use of the stack. For example, instead of promoting a **short** to an **int** before passing it, the compiler can just put a **short** on the stack, and the routine can expect that the stack only has a **short**, not an **int**. This lowers the overhead of calling such a function, especially because it can eliminate the promotion of a **float** to a **double**.

However, since the users of your library can compile their code with or without prototypes but your library must be compiled only one of these ways, you must make sure that the types of your parameters will be the same in either case. This means that you cannot write a function that expects a **short**, **char**, or **float**, since the nonprototyped compiler will promote them and the prototyped one may not. You must restrict yourself to nonpromoted types (**int**, **long**, their **signed** and **unsigned** flavors, **double**, **struct**, **union**, and any pointer type) for library function parameters. The ANSI committee faced this problem, too, which is why all prototypes for the standard's library functions follow this restriction.

Your other option is to provide two libraries, one each for pre-ANSI and ANSI environments. This is a major hassle, but might be worth it for libraries that took lots of **float** parameters in time-critical functions, since converting a **double** to a **float** can be expensive. If you decide to do this, make sure you realize how much pain you will cause in terms of maintaining and documenting your environment.

You might also notice that we used an identifier beginning with an underscore after telling you that these are reserved and should be avoided. This is an interesting point: our library is not part of the ANSI system, but it also must interact with user's code and, when installed, is in some sense part of the user's system. Since users are not supposed to use identifiers starting with _, this guarantees that we don't conflict with their symbols, but puts us in jeopardy of conflicting with the local system's symbols. I figure that whoever ports the library to a new system will change the identifier to a nonconflicting one, and this is cleaner than telling all application writers who use your library to avoid some identifier because you use it for internal, arcane reasons.

5.5.4 Widened Types in Functions

Functions that rely on widening of types smaller than **int** to **int** width, or **float** to **double**, will get a rude shock when they are compiled under ANSI, because under ANSI the widened type is converted back to the narrower one inside the function. The most common form of this is to assume that your **float** parameters really have **double** precision. You might, for example, have pre-ANSI code that passes a pointer to its so-called **float** parameter into a function that expects a **double ***:

```
dibble(fval)
float   fval;
{
        pr_dbl_list(1, &fval);
}
```

```
pr_dbl_list(cnt, dp)
int     cnt;
double  *dp;
{
        /* ... */
}
```

What is really wrong here is that `fval` never really *was* a `float`; it was just declared to be one, and the compiler silently treated it as a `double`. This meant that you could use a pointer to it for routines that expected a `double *` and get away with it. Because this is pre-ANSI code, there is no prototype. Thus, when you compile it on an ANSI system, the compiler will not complain about the mismatch between the `float *` from `&fval` and the `double *` that `pr_dbl_list()` expects, and `pr_dbl_list()` will probably fail spectacularly, trying to use a `float` as if it were a `double`. Such code is too ugly to live anyway, and should be fixed forthwith; I don't want to hear any whining about this at all.

5.5.5 struct

You can pass a `struct` as a parameter, and functions can return a `struct` (this was true in many compilers already, but not all).

5.6 Initialization

5.6.1 Old-Style Initialization Vanishing

ANSI has made the = mandatory in an initialization. Old-style initialization left it out:

```
int     i 0;
```

This is another one of those things that's been hanging around C for years, like that moldy eggplant in your refrigerator, and ANSI finally got brave enough to pick it up and throw it out.

5.6.2 union

Current C compilers generally do not let you initialize a `union`, the argument being that they don't know which member of the `union` you are trying to initialize. Many solutions have been proposed for this, including deciding by the type of the initializer. This could get pretty hairy (is 2 a `short` or a `long`?), so ANSI picked a simple mechanism — initializers set the first listed member. This is simpleminded, but quite predictable. For example, in the following code `v.i` is initialized to 12.

```
typedef union {
        int     i;
        char    *str;
        double  d;
} value;
```

```
value    v = { 12 };
```

5.6.3 auto Initialization

Auto aggregate initialization is now supported. Or, if you'd like me to speak in English, you can now initialize a nonstatic **struct**, **union**, or array in a function. For example, you could always say

```
typedef struct {
        char    *name;
        int     value;
} ENTRY;

void
my_function()
{
        static ENTRY    Who_am_i = {
                              "nobody", 0
                        };

        /* ... */
}
```

Although many compilers still will not let you do it, in ANSI C the following is legal:

```
void
my_function()
{
        ENTRY   who_are_you[] = {
                        "somebody",     1000,
                        "everybody",    10000,
                };

        /* ... */
}
```

Such variables are called *automatic* or *auto* variables, and the **auto** keyword allows you to be explicit about this if you want. (**auto** is an old C feature, not a new ANSI one.)

5.7 Scoping Rules

5.7.1 extern

Many pre-ANSI C implementations remember external declarations, especially function declarations, outside of their block scope. For example, take the following code:

```
tick()
{
        extern double   sqrt();

        /* ... */
}

tock()
{
        double  d;

        d = sqrt(15.0);
}
```

In many current C implementations the code inside **tock()** would still know that **sqrt()** returns a **double**. In ANSI, this is not true, because the block containing the initial declaration has gone out of scope. Since it isn't remembered, the **sqrt()** inside **tock()** will be thought to return an **int**, which will give you gibberish. A thoughtful compiler might warn you about this, but such a warning is not required.

5.7.2 struct and union Tags

It has long been legal to have a structure declaration without a body. This is necessary for a forward reference to a structure that must be defined later. For example, two structures that point at each other would need to be declared like this:

```
struct tweedledee;        /* say that such a struct exists */

struct tweedledum {
        struct tweedledee       *tp;
        /* ... */
};

struct tweedledee {
        struct tweedledum       *tp;
        /* ... */
};
```

Almost all existing compilers would accept this already. But a new meaning has been added to such an empty declaration — it hides any structure definition under the same tag in an outer block. This allows you to reuse or hide a structure tag. For example, if the **struct** code above were included inside a block, and the structure **tweedledee** had a different meaning outside the block, most current compilers would have no way of expressing the fact that the reference used in **tweedledum** was to the newly defined **tweedledee** instead of the one defined outside the block.

This is garbage, of course. You shouldn't *ever* do this except at gunpoint, any more than you should define your own **printf()** routine with different semantics. There are lots of possible identifier names, and I guarantee that not all of the good ones are taken. You will only confuse people if you override type names. The only time I can imagine using this is if there are conflicting names in files you don't control, in which case you may need this to be able to work with both of them. If you must do this, comment voluminously.

5.8 External Variables

One change has been made related to global external variables that makes a reasonably common practice not portable. In many C compilers, global variables without initializers do not need the **extern** keyword. For example, you could have the declaration

```
int     Num_gerbils;
```

in a header file that was included in many source files. When the loader[4] came to put all the files together, if there had been no explicitly initialized declaration the loader would create a variable initialized to zero. In contrast,

```
extern int      Num_gerbils;
```

in the header would, by itself, never force space to be allocated.

In ANSI, having multiple non-**extern** declarations of the same variable in different files is not portable. What the compiler does with this is undefined, so existing environments may continue to work as they do now; you just can't rely on it. The header file would have to contain the **extern** version, and exactly one source file would have an initialization, either explicitly providing a value or defaulting to zero with a simple

```
int     Num_gerbils;
```

By the bye, **extern** declarations can now have initializers. For example, we could have said

```
extern int      Num_gerbils = 13;
```

(again, as long as this only happened in one source file).

This aspect of external variables was one of the larger areas of discussion in the ANSI committee, since there were two incompatible existing practices. Whichever ANSI picked would break the other, so they picked the one easiest to implement on the most machines.

Some compilers allow you to forward reference `static` variables just as you would **extern** variables. For example, you could have

```
static double   scales[];

        /* ... */
        v *= scales[cur_scale];
        /* ... */

static double   scales[] = {
                            0.25, 0.5, 1.0, 2.0
                        };
```

In ANSI, you may not have a `static` variable of unknown size, so this kind of forward reference is illegal.

[4] A common UNIX-related term, "loader" is the word we use when other people might say "link-editor".

5.9 Summary

By this point you may be wondering what ANSI was thinking of when they made all these changes, and whether you should turn them in to the FBI for recreational drug use. I would recommend not doing so. In fact, almost everything you know about types is still correct. The basic types have not changed; `struct`, `union`, and (for all practical purposes) `enum` have not changed; the old-style function parameter definition is still accepted (as long as it doesn't conflict with a prototype, if there is one); and so on. There have only been minor changes in existing behavior, and the addition of some useful mechanisms. If you still have a hankering to turn someone in, try turning in those know-it-alls who were asking about prototypes for functions without arguments. That should teach 'em a lesson.

Chapter 6 Expressions

6.1 Parentheses and Order of Operation

Order of operation is one of those sticky points that seems monumentally picayune, but is really sometimes your only defense against underflow or overflow, so pay attention.

Let's take for our text the expression

```
f1() * (f2() * f3())
```

The compiler might rewrite this internally as

```
vf1 = f1();
vf2 = f2();
vf3 = f3();
vf1 * (vf2 * vf3)
```

where `vf1`, `vf2`, and `vf3` are compiler-invented temporary variables.

In K&R, order of evaluation in an expression was unspecified. The compiler was free to do the three assignments in its internal form in any order it wanted — you had no guarantee about the order in which the functions would be called. Further, since theoretically it makes no difference what order you multiply numbers in, the compiler might multiply `vf1 * vf2` before multiplying by `vf3`. The problem was that expressions are not evaluated theoretically: they are evaluated on real machines with fixed word sizes. So the order in which operations are carried out can be critical to avoiding overflow and underflow. If you wanted to control the order of evaluation, you had to introduce temporary variables, breaking up the expression into multiple assignments.

ANSI has not changed the fact that the compiler may call the functions in any order. What *is* now guaranteed is that the order of operations will obey the parentheses, that is, that `(vf2 * vf3)` will be done, and the result will be multiplied by `vf1`.

Why should you care? Well, if `vf1` and `vf2` were very large, and `vf3` were fractional, it might make a difference, since `vf1 * vf2` might overflow, but if `vf2 * vf3` were done first, the resulting value, when multiplied by `vf1` might not. In such situations as this, order of operation can be critical. In many instances it is completely invisible to the user, including its effect on efficiency. This should not make a program less efficient except that the compiler is now no longer quite as free to pre-evaluate constant parts of expressions.

6.2 Sequence Points

ANSI has formalized a point of some minor divergence in compilers, namely, when side effects are guaranteed to have happened. A compiler usually guarantees that side effects (such as `++` produces) will have been completed before certain *sequence points* are passed. The operators that provide sequence points in ANSI are `,` (comma), `&&`, `||`, and the `?` in a `?:` (that is, a `?:` expression). A *full expression* (an expression that is not part of any other expression, for example, a semicolon-terminated expression) is also a sequence point. For the most part this is just a formalization of how most compilers did things, but some compilers were a little more flexible, and a few were less. (Note that we are talking about the comma *operator*, not the comma as used to separate function arguments, which is not a sequence point.) For example, look at the following code:

```
i = 0;
array[i] = i++;
```

After it is executed, `i` will have the value `1`, because we will have crossed the sequence point of the second semicolon. However, the second statement might set either `array[0]` or `array[1]` since there is no sequence point between `i++` and its use as an array subscript. A compiler might evaluate the right-hand side of the assignment either before or after the left, giving different results.

6.3 Sign-Preserving Rules

In many existing C implementations, the `unsigned` modifier was quite sticky. It spread across expressions, contaminating all integral types with which it came in contact. For example, given

```
unsigned short  u;
short           i, j;

u = 6;
j = -3;

i = u / j;
```

in the final expression both `u` and `j` would be widened to `unsigned int`, the expression would be evaluated, and the result stored in `i`. This is called *sign-preserving* evaluation.

However, other C compilers would (if a `short` was smaller than an `int`) have converted both to a signed `int`, since it was big enough to hold any unsigned value of a `short`. This is called *value-preserving* evaluation.

In ANSI C, what will happen is that all expressions will have their *value* preserved, rather than their *unsignedness*. This is most intuitive; in our example above, `u / j` should probably equal -2, not (with a compiler with a 32-bit `int`) 4294967294. However, programs that rely on the unsigned-preserving behavior will undergo a quiet change. This quiet change is considered to be the nastiest one introduced.

This difference is no difference at all, except when both the following conditions prevail:

(1) An expression with an unsigned type smaller than an `int` results in an `int`-wide value with the sign bit set; and

(2) The result of the expression is used where its sign is significant because (a) the expression must be widened to a `long` on an implementation where `int` is smaller than `long`; (b) it is the left-hand side of a `>>` in an environment that does sign extension on such a shift; (c) it is an operand of `<`, `>`, `<=`, `>=`, `/`, or `%`; or (d) it is assigned to a floating-point type.

There is also a possible problem when you have a binary operator with one unsigned integer and one negative signed integer. In this case, if the signed `int` is treated as an unsigned bit pattern, it will suddenly become a very large number.

Although this may seem strange, it actually eliminates a few weird cases. For example, in pre-ANSI C, the result of subtracting an unsigned `(unsigned short) 5`, say, from `(unsigned short) 3` could be another large unsigned number that had the same bit representation as -2 on that machine. This was conceptually bizarre. In ANSI C, the result is `(signed int) -2`. If you assign it to an unsigned integer you will see no difference, but if you store it in a signed integer, no conversion (real *or* conceptual) will be necessary to get the intuitive result.

This all sounds really picayune. Let's look at an example where it makes a critical difference. Suppose we had a fragment of code for a machine with a 16-bit `int` that was used to move nuclear fuel rods into the reactor core.

```
# define        UP      0x0001
# define        DOWN    0xffff  /* integer -1? */

# define        DELTA(amount,dir)       ((amount) * (dir))

        /* move rod halfway in */
        move_rod(DELTA(0.5, DOWN));
```

Instead of moving the rod partway down into the core to slow down the nuclear reaction, the `move_rod()` call above will yank the rod completely out, since `DOWN`, as a hex constant, will be `unsigned int`, not (as the comment assumes) `-1`. If you use hex or octal constants to represent negative values, you will get in this kind of trouble all the time, and *you* will have to call the governor and explain the cause of the meltdown.

6.4 float Expressions

In K&R, the only actual floating-point type was `double`. The type `float` really only existed as a space saver. Even in expressions involving only `float`, each `float` would always be converted to a `double`, the operation(s) would be performed, and the result converted back. ANSI C allows expressions involving only `floats` to be evaluated at the reduced precision. This speeds up such calculations, sometimes enormously, at the cost of a quiet change, since the result may be slightly (or in some complicated cases very) different. This is a quiet change that is surely worth it. I say this with the confidence of having no code that would be affected by it.

6.5 Function Pointers

Most people are accustomed to using a function pointer like this:

```
void    (*fp)(const char *);

fp = atoi;       /* get the address of the atoi() function */

(*fp)(value);
```

ANSI has added a somewhat common syntax

```
fp(value);
```

This makes function pointers syntactically analogous to other pointers; for example, compare and contrast the new syntax with

```
int     *ip;

ip = int_array; /* get the address of the int_array "array" */

ip[i] = 0;
```

In the `int *` case, to get a pointer to an array, you simply name the array. To use it, you use an implicit indirection operator. The old function pointer syntax let you get the address by simply naming the function, but to use it you had to use explicit indirection (it is even arguable that there was a double indirection: one explicit (the `*`) and the other implicit (the parameter list)). In any case, the new syntax is more consistent with this paradigm. Both syntaxes are still supported.

6.6 Unary Plus

ANSI has also added a unary plus operator, so that you can have `+3` as a constant, being explicit about its sign. If this thrills you, you must have a very boring life. I have also wondered for quite a while why they added this for symmetry, but failed to add a logical exclusive-or operator `^^`, so that the list of bitwise operators (`&`, `|`, `^`) was fully matched by the logical operators (`&&`, `||`, `^^`). Besides, I've actually wanted `^^` on occasion, and have had to code around its absence, but I've never had to write uglier code because I didn't have unary plus.

6.7 Old-Style Operators Vanishing

The original assignment operators in C used to have the operator following the equal sign. For example, instead of

```
x -= 42;
```

you would have typed

```
x =- 42;
```

The order was switched to avoid the ambiguity of expressions without spaces, such as

```
x=-42;
```

which could either have subtracted `42` from `x`, or set `x` to `-42`. ANSI has finally (yea!) eliminated the old style of assignment operator. Existing code that let the compiler use the old style to disambiguate the expression above will find that it now has the assignment meaning. This will be a quiet change, but frankly if you haven't fixed this type of code by now you probably deserve it. This change is ancient history, and compilers have been generating warnings for over a decade. If you never listened to your compiler about this, you probably never listened to your mother either, and deserve everything that happens to you.

6.8 Left-Hand-Side Casts

Some compilers allowed you to put casts on the left-hand side of an assignment operator. This is no longer allowed.

Some of you will be more unhappy than you might think, since there is an unobvious consequence: you cannot use casts to change the size for incrementing a pointer. For example, the following code which relies on left-hand-side casts will no longer work:

```
copy(
        char    *s1,
        char    *s2,
        size_t  len
)
{
        for (; len >= sizeof (long); len -= sizeof (long))
                *((long *) s1)++ = *((long *) s2)++;
        for (; len > 0; len--)  /* copy trailing few bytes */
                *s1++ = *s2++;
}
```

This kind of code, which uses a pointer to a larger type in order to copy more bytes per iteration, would have to be rewritten to use an actual pointer variable of type `long` instead of just casting its input pointers.

6.9 ?: (the Conditional Operator)

The `?:` operator (called the *conditional operator*) has been expanded in use. It was always able to take standard arithmetic expressions for the second and third expressions (sometimes called the *result* expressions). ANSI now allows **`void`**, **`struct`**, or **`union`** as valid types. It is still true that if the types of the result expressions differ, the compiler will use standard conversions to promote one to the type of the other (the new type being the type of the entire conditional expression). If it can't do so (for example, if the result expressions are of different **`struct`** types), the expression is invalid. This means that, if one expression is a pointer, the other may be a **`void *`**, which will be automatically cast to the pointer type of the other result expression, making it the type of the overall expression.

6.10 The Shift Operators

Many existing compilers viewed the right-hand operand of the shift operators << and >> as any other operand when it came to typing an expression. This meant that such expressions as

```
(1 << 16L)
```

would be of type `long`. ANSI found this bogus; the left-hand side of a shift operator is the type of the expression. This is a quiet change in some cases. For instance, on a machine with a 16-bit `int` and a 32-bit `long`, our example above would evaluate to `0`, not `0x10000L`.

6.11 % (Modulo)

The `%` operator now only works with integral types. Some compilers would accept this with floating-point types; ANSI C makes this illegal. They say this is because it duplicates `fmod()`, which impresses me not at all. Consistency is more important than a minor duplication of this type — `%` is the only arithmetic operator that doesn't accept floating-point types.

Chapter 7 Statements

7.1 switch

A `switch` statement is no longer evaluated solely as an `int`, but, based on the type of the controlling expression (the one on the `switch` line between the parentheses), may also be evaluated as a `long`. All `case` labels are converted to the controlling expression's type.

This results in another silent change, by the way, in that existing `switch` statements that *rely* on truncation of `long case` labels to `int` will get different results. I say good riddance; this is a major crock anyway.

Some compilers would accept pointer types for the controlling expression and pointer constants for the `case` labels. This is not legal in ANSI C.

Besides this, there are no changes in statements in ANSI C. You have now finished the shortest chapter in the book.

Chapter 8 Future Language Directions

The ANSI standard contains several statements of future expectations for the language's direction. They take the forms of warnings against relying on some deprecated features, and some guidance to people who might want to extend in certain directions. You are advised to take heed if you want your programs to continue to work in future versions of ANSI C. The future direction statements are:

(1) The limit of six-character monocase names for external identifiers was a "concession to existing implementations". Presumably later revisions of the standard will ease this. It can't happen soon enough for me.

(2) Putting storage class specifiers anywhere but at the beginning of a declaration "is an obsolescent feature". This means that, although ANSI didn't make the following illegal:

```
int static      kilroy_was_here = TRUE;
```

it would have liked to, and might do so in the future.

(3) Declarations or definitions of functions in the nonprototyped old style will certainly go away someday. I wouldn't hold my breath, though.

(4) If a function has two parameters declared with array (not pointer) type, passing in the same object for both "is an obsolescent feature". For example, given

```
void
vector_multiply(
        int     length,
        double  vector1[],
        double  vector2[],
        double  result_vector[]
);
```

you should not call **vector_multiply()** with any two of the array parameters referring to overlapping parts of the same array.

The idea is that, in the future, a vectorizing compiler would be able to take advantage of this knowledge and generate stupendously fast code. Of course, as you might notice, it would preclude saying "multiply **v1** by **v2**" in the following, obvious fashion:

```
vector_multiply(100, v1, v2, v1);
```

(5) ANSI has reserved for future use as character escape sequences all lowercase letters preceded by a \. They also warn that characters coming after a new escape sequence may be used as extenders (just as **\x** uses any following hex digits as extenders). As a general rule, if you want the character \ you should use \\, so that any future changes to the escape sequence set won't change the meanings of your character strings.

Library

Chapter 9 Library

The ANSI committee was faced with a rather interesting task when it came to the library routines. C without library routines is basically useless, since its I/O mechanisms are part of its library, not part of the language, and a program with neither input nor output is not likely to be of great benefit to humanity.[1] Also, a large number of routines have become part of the programming environment on which C programmers have come to rely.

However, the divergence of behavior and "syntax" (that is, parameter order and meaning) is much greater here than in the C language. There are two major branches of development with sometimes widely diverging mechanisms, namely System V and Version 7 (from which much of the BSD library is derived). But each of these branches, especially Version 7, has its own divergences within the family. ANSI started from the */usr/group Standard* which mostly codified System V behavior when it differed from Version 7 derivates. ANSI created a lot more new stuff for the library than was added in the language, including several new header files and quite a few new functions. It explicitly does not define OS-specific calls, such as **read()** and **write()**, but either uses variants for which portable semantics are describable (such as **fread()** and **fwrite()**) or considers them completely outside the scope of the ANSI standard (functions like **chdir()** or (shudder) **stat()**).

Almost all library functions are allowed to have a "safe" macro version (one that evaluates each parameter exactly once), but must have, unless otherwise stated, a real function form that can have its address taken. This means that library functions can normally be executed as inline functions, but must have a real function version whose address can be passed to routines that need a function pointer. The way you guarantee that you are dealing with the real function and not a macro is to **#undef** the macro name like this:

[1] It should be noted that being a benefit to humanity is not, per se, a requirement for strictly conforming programs.

```
#undef strcmp
qsort(strings, num_strings, sizeof *strings, strcmp);
```

For historical reasons, there are two exceptions to this — `getc()` and `putc()` — which are allowed to be unsafe with the stream argument; that is, it may be evaluated more than once.

All library prototypes use widened types. See Section 5.5.3 above to tell you why the committee did this, and why, if you are writing your own library header files, you should, too.

Chapter 10 <stddef.h>

The new header file `<stddef.h>` defines several widely used types and macros, namely:

`NULL`
: A generic pointer constant guaranteed not to point to anything valid (so it can be used to denote an improper or unallocated pointer). A compiler is not required to catch invalid use of a `NULL` pointer; this is an area of undefined behavior.

`offsetof(structure,field)`
: A macro that returns the offset of a given *field* within a specified *structure* type. This can be useful (together with `sizeof`) for writing data structures to files in a table-driven way by constructing a table of the offset and the size of each structure member that must be saved, and then handing that table, and a pointer to an object to be saved, to a generic routine which can then handle saving or restoring any structure with such a description (see below for an example of how this might be done). Not surprisingly, this macro will not work with bitfields, which cannot have their addresses taken.

`ptrdiff_t`
: A signed integer type guaranteed to hold the result of a valid subtraction of two pointers.

`size_t`
: The unsigned integer type of a `sizeof`, that is, a type big enough to hold the largest declarable object on the system. Parameters to `malloc()` are now of type `size_t`. It is always a good idea to use `size_t` instead of `long` or `int` to hold sizes of objects, since it will make your programs much more portable.

`wchar_t`
: The type of a wide character constant. It is guaranteed to be integral, but nothing

else is guaranteed. Constants like `L'\xA1'` are of type `wchar_t`. This semi-official status for `wchar_t` is odd, since a compiler construct generates constants of a non-built-in type. At some future time `wchar_t` or some replacement type may become an official part of the language.

As an example of using `offsetof()`, suppose we wanted to create a mechanism for writing parts of structures to files. Here is what the main part of the header file might look like (we have left off handling conditional prototypes, C++ mechanisms, and multiple inclusion to concentrate on what's important to the example):

```
# include       <stddef.h>

typedef struct {
        char    *name;          /* for debug purposes */
        size_t  offset, size;
} field;

/* Create a field entry from the type and element names */
# define FIELD_ENTRY(type,n) {                          \
                        #n, offsetof(type,n),           \
                        sizeof ((type *) NULL)->n       \
                }

int     write_struct(
                void    *entry,
                field   desc[],
                size_t  num_fields,
                FILE    *fp
        );

int     read_struct(
                void    *entry,
                field   desc[],
                size_t  num_fields,
                FILE    *fp
        );
```

Each `field` structure describes a single structure field, with its name, offset from the beginning, and size (the name is useful for debugging). Users could use arrays of `field` structures to describe the parts of their structures they wanted to save in a file, and then use `write_struct()` to store a single structure, and `read_struct()` to read it back out. For example, for a linked list of graph points, the user's code might look like this:

```
typedef struct val_ {
        double          value;
        short           x, y;
        struct val_     *next;
} val;
```

```
field   val_desc[] = {
                FIELD_ENTRY(val, value),
                FIELD_ENTRY(val, x),
                FIELD_ENTRY(val, y),
        };

const size_t val_cnt = sizeof val_desc / sizeof val_desc[0];

val     *Vlist;
FILE    *Store;

save()
{
        val     *vp;

        for (vp = Vlist; vp != NULL; vp = vp->next)
                write_struct(vp, val_desc, val_cnt, Store);
}

restore()
{
        val     *vp;
        val     cur;

        Vlist = NULL;
        while (read_struct(&cur, val_desc, val_cnt, Store)) {
                vp = (val *) malloc(sizeof *vp);
                *vp = cur;
                vp->next = Vlist;       /* insert at beginning */
                Vlist = vp;
        }
}
```

Because we reconstruct the list at restore time, and because the order of the list is not important to this program, there is no need for `save()` and `restore()` to read or write the `next` field to the file. The list is simply rebuilt in `restore()`.

Chapter 11 <stdio.h>

The header file `<stdio.h>` is an old friend. It defines almost all the standard I/O routines any maximally portable program should be using. You should avoid using the lower-level UNIX calls such as `open()`, `read()`, and `close()`. In essence, `fopen()` and friends are much more portable than the UNIX `open()` and company. Even in cases of inefficiency, if you can stand it you should stick with the standard I/O versions of routines, since they are portable. Pressure from users (such as you) might get vendors to enhance their implementations.

`<stdio.h>` provides functions to perform operations on files, on data contained in files (including formatted I/O routines and positioning), and to handle errors associated with using files.

11.1 Operations on Files

ANSI provides an `int remove(const char *file)` function which takes a file name as a parameter and removes it, returning zero on success; all other values indicate failure. On UNIX systems this translates directly to the `unlink()` system call.

The now-common UNIX atomic renaming function `int rename(const char *from, const char *to)` has been codified by the standard. The exact behavior is implementation defined, since non-UNIX systems may not have an actual atomic rename call. It returns zero on success; all other values indicate failure.

A new function `FILE *tmpfile(void)` returns a pointer to a file opened with the mode `"wb+"` that will be removed when it is closed or when the program exits normally (abnormal exit may or may not remove the file). This is obviously useful for the program that needs a temporary file for storing data.

The new function `char *tmpnam(char *buf)` fills in the data space pointed to by `buf` with a unique temporary file name. The buffer should be at least `L_tmpnam` `chars` long. If `buf` is `NULL`, `tmpnam()` returns a pointer to static data which might be modified on subsequent calls, so it should be saved to guarantee its state. Otherwise it simply returns `buf`. This differs from `mktemp()` (which the standard does not provide, although it may be familiar to old UNIX hands) by not allowing the user to set the template for temporary file names. File names are arbitrarily chosen by `tmpnam()`, and they are of no guaranteed pattern.

`tmpnam()` gives more control than `tmpfile()`, but since other programs may call `tmpnam()` between the time you call it and the time you try to use the name, your code should be robust for the file already existing by the time you try to use it.

11.2 File Access Functions

`fflush()` now can have a `NULL` parameter as its file pointer, in which case it will flush all buffers of all open files. This is useful in routines such as signal handlers which want to make sure that all output has been flushed without having to figure out which files are open. They can simply call `fflush(NULL)` and be done with it.

`fopen()` has a new mode `b` for "binary", which stops all interpretation of the file's bytes. For example, the canonical standard I/O model says that file lines are terminated with newlines (`\n`). On a system that uses carriage-return/line-feeds (commonly called CRLF) to delimit lines, a normal `fopen()` will make this fact invisible to the I/O routines, whereas `fopen()` with mode `b` will expose it.

The `fopen()` append mode specifier `a` makes *all* writes append to the end of the file, regardless of file positioning via `fseek()` or any other method. If you want to be able to move around arbitrarily in a file, you must open it with `r` and, if that fails because the file doesn't exist, open it with `w`. On BSD (and many other Version 7-type systems), `a` meant to open the file if it existed, create it if it didn't, and then seek to the end; it did not force all writes to append. This is a quiet change for you BSD types, one that is likely to be quite deadly.

A file opened for both reading and writing must have a call to some positioning function (`fseek()`, `fsetpos()`, `rewind()`, or `fflush()`) before switching between reading and writing. This is necessary on some existing operating systems, although I don't know why ANSI didn't make this stuff the responsibility of library implementors. One presumes that routines can remember whether the last operation on a `FILE *` was a read or a write operation, and make any necessary calls required by the system when changing modes. I have no idea why this has been left to the poor user to do all the time instead of having implementors on such systems handle it internally. The best no-op version of this is

```
fseek(stream, 0L, SEEK_CUR);
```

which says, "Seek to zero bytes from my current position".

The `setbuf()` call is subsumed by `setvbuf()`, but is still available for compatibility.

If the `setvbuf()` call is used, it must be called before any I/O is done on a given stream. It was adopted from System V. Its signature is

```
int
setvbuf(
        FILE    *stream,
        char    *buf,
        int     mode,
        size_t  size
);
```

The valid values for **mode** are **_IOFBUF** for fully buffered I/O; **_IOLBUF** for line-buffered I/O; **_IONBUF** for unbuffered I/O. If **buf** isn't **NULL**, the implementation is allowed (but not required) to use it for buffering; **size** is the buffer's size. The function returns zero on success.

BSD people should note that the **setlinebuf()** call is *not* provided for compatibility; after all, it isn't System V so why should they care? If *you* care, here is a macro to map it to the ANSI equivalent:

```
# define        setlinebuf(stream)   setvbuf(stream, NULL, _IOLBF, 0)
```

11.3 Formatted I/O

11.3.1 printf()

The **printf()** family (**printf()**, **fprintf()**, **sprintf()**, **vprintf()**, **vfprintf()**, and **vsprintf()**) has acquired some new behavior and formats. They are:

%Lf Print out a **long double**. The **L** modifier also works with the other floating-point formats (**e**, **E**, **g**, and **G**).

%p Print out a **void *** pointer in an implementation-specific format which, if you're lucky, the **scanf()** variant will read back in properly. You should live so long.

%n This new format means that the argument is a pointer to an integer that will be filled in with the number of characters output so far with this call. It is useful for keeping track of your place in your overall output stream. (By default, this is an **int**, unless the **n** is preceded by the usual modifiers **l** for **long** or **h** for **short**.) An example of its use is given below.

%g The ANSI standard specifies that **%g** switches from floating-point format to an exponential format at an exponent of -4; some existing implementations use -3 instead. This is a very trivial quiet change.

%i Equivalent to **%d**. This is provided for compatibility with **scanf()** (see below).

The most useful addition, as well as the most counterintuitive, is the **%n** format. It is useful in that it allows you to keep track of where you are in the output, and it is counter-intuitive, since it stores a value rather than printing one. For example, you could write a routine that avoids hitting the right-hand edge of the terminal in something like the following manner:

```
void
flow_out(
        double  value,
        char    *tag
)
{
        int     end;

        printf("The current flow value is %f%n", value, &end);
        if (end + strlen(tag) >= TERMINAL_WIDTH)
                printf("\n\t");
        else
                printf(" ");
        printf("%s\n", tag);
}
```

The `%n` at the end of the first `printf()`'s format will put the number of characters output into the variable `end`. Then, if adding the tag would force us past the end of the terminal's line, we start an indented new line for the tag; otherwise we just put the tag on the same line.

`printf()` returns the number of characters printed by the command, which can also be useful. In fact, the example above for `%n` could have been written using that return value instead.

For some of you the `v` (variable argument) forms of the `printf()` functions (namely `vprintf()`, `vfprintf()`, and `vsprintf()`) may be new. They are just `printf()` for which the arguments after the format are passed as a single `va_list` pointer. See the description of `<stdarg.h>` below (Chapter 15) for an example of how to use these routines.

The functions `ecvt()`, `fcvt()`, and `gcvt()` have been eliminated in favor of `sprintf()`. They are trivially writable as calls to `sprintf()`, and they are used in very little code, so it was felt that the redundancy wasn't worth the rarely needed upward compatibility.

11.3.2 scanf()

The `scanf()` functions (`scanf()`, `fscanf()`, and `sscanf()`) also have the new `%n` option, in this case for the number of characters scanned so far.

The new `%i` allows you to scan integer constants with C-style syntax to determine the base (decimal, octal, or hex). In other words, `%i` recognizes constants of the form `03476`, `62586`, `0x8ba74d`, and so forth.

There are no `v` (variable argument) forms of `scanf()`. The committee decided they didn't like `scanf()` much, and wanted to discourage its use. Thanks a lot, folks. If you create a general data-file writing routine using formats with `vfprintf()`, it would be nice to be able to write a general data-file *reading* routine that passed the same formats to `vsscanf()`. But `scanf()` offends their tender sensibilities, so you just have to live without it. I know that some vendors are providing these anyway; we can only hope that the next version of the standard fills this gap.

The function `isspace()` is now used by `scanf()` to define what constitutes white space, which is affected by the new stuff (see Chapter 23).

11.4 Character I/O

ungetc() can be implemented in lots of ways. All the ANSI standard guarantees is that you can push back a different character than the last one you read. You cannot rely on being able to push back more than one character at a time. Nor can you rely on the file position being meaningful after an **ungetc()** until all ungotten characters are read back. Any successful calls to **fseek()**, **rewind()**, or **fsetpos()** will discard any pending characters pushed back with **ungetc()**.

Implementations are not required to allow more than one character to be pushed back; a failed **ungetc()** returns **EOF**. If your program relies on pushing back more than one character, it may break on some systems. Characters will be read back in a last-in-first-out order.

ungetc() can now be called even if no characters have been read from a stream.

11.5 Direct I/O

Parameters to **fread()** and **fwrite()** regarding size are now of type **size_t**.

11.6 File Positioning

Two new functions, **int fgetpos(FILE *stream, fpos_t *pos)** and **int fsetpos(FILE *stream, const fpos_t *pos)** allow you to get and set the position of a file without assuming that a file position is equivalent to a **long**, which the **ftell()** and **fseek()** functions assume. Both new functions return zero if successful; all other values indicate failure. Here is an example of their use:

```
int
add_to_file(
        FILE    *fp
)
{
        fpos_t  cur_pos;
        char    data;

        fgetpos(fp, &cur_pos);
        while ((data = get_data()) != DONE)
                if (data == ERROR) {
                        /* back up over written data to */
                        /* undo this add_to_file() */
                        fsetpos(fp, &cur_pos);
                        return ERROR;
                }
                else
                        putc(data, fp);
        return DONE;
}
```

11.7 Error Handling

The function `void clearerr(FILE *)` clears any error conditions on a given stream. Of course, this doesn't mean it makes the actual error go away (for that you need your Fairy Godmother); it clears the error flags set in the given stream descriptor so you can test them later to see if they have reappeared.

See Section 13.3 below for a description of `strerror()`, a string-returning variant of `perror()`.

Chapter 12 <ctype.h>

The conversion functions `toupper()` and `tolower()` are now guaranteed to return their input character unless there is a lower- or uppercase equivalent. This means they are safe to call without calling `islower()` or `isupper()` first. Some current implementations just assume their inputs are upper- or lowercase, forcing you to check first. In other words, code that looks like this:

```
if (isupper(ch))
        ch = tolower(ch);
```

can safely be rewritten simply as

```
ch = tolower(ch);
```

All functions except `isdigit()` and `isxdigit()` are affected by the locale mechanism (see Chapter 23).

12.1 Reserved Identifiers

The committee thinks it might someday want to use other identifiers starting with `is` or `to` followed by lowercase letters, so it kindly requests you to keep your grubby paws off them.

Chapter 13 <string.h>

This header file contains prototypes for functions that manipulate memory as sequences of bytes. There are two kinds of such functions, those that view memory as blocks of bytes of a given length, and those that understand byte strings terminated with a null byte (`'\0'`).

For both kinds of functions, any comparisons are done as `unsigned char`, not the compiler's default `char`.

`strcoll()` and `strxfrm()` are new functions dealing with the locale-specific stuff. See the description in Chapter 23 below.

13.1 Block Memory Functions

ANSI has adopted the `mem` block memory-handling functions, and has added one new one. All these functions deal with blocks of a given size, pointed at by a `void *`.

```
void *
memcpy(void *dest, const void *src, size_t size)
```

Copy the `src` block to the `dest` block. The two blocks must not overlap. Returns `dest`.

```
void *
memmove(void *dest, const void *src, size_t size)
```

Like `memcpy()`, but works for overlapping blocks of memory, which `memcpy()` is now allowed to mishandle in the interest of speed. Don't rely on your system's `memcpy()` getting overlapping blocks right. For example, if you have code that attempts to shift blocks around to insert new data, using `memcpy()` is hazardous. For example, the following code should not be done with `memcpy()`:

```
insert(
        int     *data,
        size_t  data_cnt,     /* current size of data */
        int     new_val,
)
{
        /* shift data right to make room for new_val */
        memmove(&data[1], data, data_cnt * sizeof data[0]);
        data[0] = new_val;
}
```

`void *`
`memset(void *block, int ch, size_t size)`

Takes `ch`, casts it to an `unsigned char`, and fills memory with the resulting value. There is no zero-explicit form à la BSD's `bzero()`, but I presume that any implementation of `memset()` could treat this as a special case if the hardware made it efficient. Returns `block`.

`void *`
`memchr(const void *block, int ch, size_t size)`

Returns a pointer to the first byte in the block with value `ch`; returns `NULL` if there is none.

`int`
`memcmp(const void *src, const void *dest, size_t size)`

Bytes are compared until they differ, and their difference is returned. If no differing bytes are found, it returns zero.

13.2 String Functions

13.2.1 String Searching Functions

For BSD and Version 7 adherents, there are several new functions with which System V people are already familiar. There is also one completely new string searching function. The new function is `strstr()`; all the others listed below are adopted System V functions.

`char *`
`strstr(const char *buf, const char *str)`

Returns a pointer to the first instance of the string `str` it finds embedded in the string `buf`.

`char *`
`strchr(const char *s, int ch)`

This is exactly equivalent to Version 7's `index()`; it returns a pointer to the first occurrence of `ch` in `str`, or `NULL` if there isn't one.

```
char *
strrchr(const char *s, int ch)
```

This is exactly equivalent to Version 7's `rindex()`; it returns a pointer to the last occurrence of `ch` in `str`, or `NULL` if there isn't one.

```
char *
strpbrk(const char *str, const char *chars)
```

Returns a pointer to the first occurrence of any character from `chars` in `str`, or `NULL` if there are none.

```
size_t
strspn(const char *str, const char *chars)
```

Returns the length of the largest initial string of `str` consisting of characters from `chars`.

```
size_t
strcspn(const char *str, const char *chars)
```

Returns the length of the largest initial string of `str` consisting of characters *not* in `chars`.

```
char *
strtok(char *str, const char *chars)
```

This function can be used to break up a string into tokens separated by strings consisting solely of the characters in `chars`. The first call to `strtok()` should pass in the pointer to the string and the separators, and will return a pointer to the first substring in its input string terminated by any of the separators, or the end of the string. On subsequent calls, a value of `NULL` for `str` means to continue on with the previous string (the set of separators in the string `chars` can vary from call to call). Calls can continue until no further string is found, when `strtok()` will return `NULL`.

A caution: `strtok()` must modify the input buffer to write null bytes at the end of tokens. If you need an unmodified version of the string, you should make a copy before you use it with `strtok()`.

As an example, the following code would process words separated by spaces and tabs:

```
char    *word, *str;

str = get_sentence();
word = strtok(str, " \t");
while (word != NULL) {
        process_word(word);
        word = strtok(NULL, " \t");
}
```

13.2.2 strcoll() and strxfrm()

ASCII, even 8-bit ASCII, is very oriented towards English, and so sorting two strings by comparing their bytes numerically works just fine for English-speaking users. However, in almost every other language in the world this will certainly fail. In French, accents on letters do not affect ordering; although ê (`'\x90'`) and é (`'\x8E'`) have different ASCII values, they should be sorted as the same letter. In Spanish, ñ (`'\x96'`) comes after `n` (`'\x6e'`) and before `o` (`'\x6f'`), although its 8-bit ASCII numerical value is on beyond `z`.

To deal with this problem, ANSI has provided two new routines.

`int`
`strcoll(const char *s1, const char *s2)`

This simply compares two strings, and, like `strcmp()` returns a value less than, equal to, or greater than zero as the first string is less than, equal to, or greater than the second. This is useful when only a few comparisons are needed on a given string, but will be slow otherwise, since it must decode on the fly locale-specific collating sequences for each string.

`size_t`
`strxfrm(char *xfrm, const char *str, size_t size)`

When you will be making several comparisons against a set of strings, `strxfrm()` is more efficient. It converts the string pointed to by `str` into a string for which the simple (and fast) `strcmp()` will give the correct answer when compared against another `strxfrm()`ed string. It puts that string into the buffer pointed at by `xfrm` (at most `size` bytes) and returns (as a `size_t`) the length of the new string. If the returned value is greater than or equal to `size`, this means that the buffer is too small (remember, the length of a string does not include the terminal `'\0'`). If `size` is zero, then `xfrm` is ignored and `strxfrm()` returns the length of the string that would be generated (so you have to add one for that null byte before allocating space for the new string).

What this means is that if you need to sort a large number of strings, you can sort them using `strcmp()` on their `strxfrm()` form, rather than using the slower `strcoll()` on the original form.

For example, take a simple phone list program that stores its data in the following structure:

```
typedef struct {
        char    *name;
        char    *phone;
        char    *xfrm;  /* used for strxfrm() */
} entry;
```

If we want to sort the names in the way the user would expect, we would first use `setlocale()` (see Chapter 23) to use the default locale's collation:

```
setlocale(LC_COLLATE, "");
```

We can then use `qsort()` to put the strings in the correct order. For the simple-but-slower case using `strcoll()`, the comparator function for `qsort()` would look like

```
int
cmp_col(
        entry   *e1,
        entry   *e2
)
{
        return strcoll(e1->name, e2->name);
}
```

For the faster-but-more-expensive variant we would need a function that precalculated the `strxfrm()` form of the string:

```
void
xfrm(
        entry   *ep
)
{
        size_t  len;

        len = strxfrm(NULL, ep->name, 0);
        ep->xfrm = (char *) malloc(len + 1);
        strxfrm(ep->xfrm, ep->name, len);
}
```

and a comparator function that used that form with the fast `strcmp()` function:

```
int
cmp_xfrm(
        entry   *e1,
        entry   *e2
)
{
        return strcmp(e1->xfrm, e2->xfrm);
}
```

Then our program could choose which one to use based on a threshold of the number of entries.

```
sort_em()
{
        entry   *names;
        size_t  num_names;
        size_t  i;

        if (num_names < THRESHOLD)
                qsort(names, num_names, sizeof *names, cmp_col);
```

```
        else {
                for (i = 0; i < num_names; i++)
                        xfrm(&names[i]);
                qsort(names, num_names, sizeof *names, cmp_xfrm);
        }
}
```

13.3 Miscellany

ANSI has added a long-needed function, **strerror(int errnum)**, which returns a string value for the given **errnum** so that user-written functions can be as nice as **perror()**. If you're using the old **sys_errlist[]** array for this purpose, cut it out right now, or I'm telling your mother.

strlen() now returns a **size_t**.

13.4 Reserved Identifiers

The ANSI standard reserves names beginning with **str** and **mem** for future use, so watch out.

Chapter 14 <stdlib.h>

The new header file `<stdlib.h>` is the dumping ground for functions that don't belong anywhere else. It defines two new types used by the integer division routines (see Section 14.6 below).

It also defines standard values to be used by `exit()`, namely `EXIT_FAILURE` and `EXIT_SUCCESS`, which you UNIX people know as nonzero and zero values for `exit()`, respectively. For maximum portability, you should start using these new values.

14.1 String Conversion

There are three new functions for converting strings to numbers. Each examines the string for a valid number, skipping over initial spaces (as defined by `isspace()`) and returns not only the converted number, but also (if you wish) a pointer to the first character in the string that follows the valid number. If there is no valid number in the input string, the routines return zero, and the "past the end" pointer (called `end` in the prototypes below), points to the beginning of the string it was passed, meaning that no characters were successfully scanned. If the input number was out of range, the return value depends on the routine (each is described below) and the variable `errno` gets set to `ERANGE` (see Chapters 18 and 21). As with all other uses of `errno`, you must explicitly set it to zero before calling the routine. For example, the complete test for errors on `strtod()` would look something like this:

```
double  val;
char    *input_buffer, *endptr;

errno = 0;
val = strtod(input_buffer, &endptr);
if (endptr == input_buffer)
        error("no valid floating-point value in input string");
else if (errno == ERANGE) {
        if (val == 0.0)
                error("value out of range: underflow");
        else
                error("value out of range: overflow");
}
else
        use_valid_value(val);
```

If the locale setting (see Chapter 23) is not `"C"`, all these routines may recognize locale-specific number representations. For example, a locale that was set for the United States might be able to read in numbers with comma separators such as `"10,000"`.

`double`
`strtod(const char *num, char **end)`
: Returns the `double` value of the string pointed to by `num`, and fills in `end` with a pointer to the first character after the value, assuming `end` is not `NULL`. If the number is out of range, `strtod()` returns ±`HUGE_VAL` (see Chapter 21). If the number would cause an underflow, it returns zero.

`long`
`strtol(const char *num, char **end, int base)`
: Converts a string to a `long`, and returns the first character after the end in `end` (if `end` is not `NULL`). It also can take a base, which, if zero, means to read in a C-style integer constant with the base encoded (that is, a leading `0x` means hex, and a leading `0` means octal), although it does not include suffixes such as `u` or `l`. `base` must be zero, or between 2 and 36. `strtol()` accepts both upper- and lowercase digits with bases greater than or equal to 10. As a special case, if the base is 16, an optional leading `0x` or `0X` may be present. On an out-of-range error, `strtol()` returns either `LONG_MIN` if the value was too small, or `LONG_MAX` if the value was too large (see Chapter 22).

`unsigned long`
`strtoul(const char *num, char **end, int base)`
: Same as `strtol()`, but returns an `unsigned long`. If the input is out of range, `strtoul()` returns `ULONG_MAX` (see Chapter 22).

14.2 Memory Allocation

Implementations differ on whether allocating a zero-length buffer returns a non-`NULL` pointer. ANSI refused to standardize on this, but did mandate that `free()` and `realloc()`

accept NULL pointers as input, thus reducing the amount of checking that needs to be done in this case. In effect, realloc() with a NULL pointer is equivalent to calling malloc(), but makes coding the initial case easier.

As an example, code that grew an array in chunks might look like the following:

```
static double   *Vals = NULL;
static long     Num_vals = 0;

# define        CHUNK   100     /* growth chunk size */

void
add_value(
        double  value
)
{
        static long     asize = 0;      /* current Vals size */

        if (Num_vals + 1 >= asize) {
                asize += CHUNK;
                Vals = (double *) realloc(Vals, asize * sizeof *Vals);
        }
        Vals[Num_vals++] = value;
}
```

If realloc() didn't treat the input value of NULL specially, the code would need an extra test for the first time a value was added.

The size parameters for all the allocation routines are of type size_t.

You System V people who are used to mucking around with the details of malloc() using the mallinfo() and mallopt() calls will be disappointed that you cannot do this portably. ANSI did not adopt them because they reveal so much of the internal workings of the routines that they would put too many constraints on implementors.

14.3 Random Numbers

The rand() function returns a value in the range 0 to RAND_MAX, a new constant guaranteed to be at least 32767. The sequence is guaranteed to be identical given the same seed to srand(), but otherwise you cannot rely on the order.

14.4 Communication with the External Environment

Even if you have a signal handler for SIGABRT, the abort() call never returns.

ANSI adopted a Whitesmith C feature called atexit(), which takes a pointer to a function with no arguments. When exit() is called, the routines registered with atexit() are called in the order of registration. This lets you have cleanup routines that get called no matter what normal termination path is followed. Unfortunately, no mechanism exists for *un*registering functions when they are no longer necessary. Sigh.

In a maximally portable program, you cannot rely on the behavior of the `system()` call except in the following limited way: `system(NULL)` returns a nonzero value if there is a command interpreter available. If there is, you can pass strings into the interpreter. The deities (if any) only know what happens to them after that. Considering that ANSI C is designed to run on systems with no UNIX heritage whatsoever, it isn't surprising that there isn't much to rely on here.

This still makes `system()` useful for passing through user commands. If you had a program that allowed the user to type a system command on a line starting with an `!` (as many interactive UNIX commands do), the fragment that handled it might look like this:

```
switch (input_line[0]) {
        /* ... */
  case '!':
        if (!system(NULL))
                printf("No command interpreter available\n");
        else
                system(&input_line[1]);
        break;
        /* ... */
}
```

14.5 Searching

A binary search routine has been added:

```
void *
bsearch(
        void    *key,
        void    *base,
        size_t  num_ele,
        size_t  size,
        int     (*compare)(const void *, const void *)
);
```

This searches a sorted array of `num_ele` elements pointed to by `base` for the given `key`. Each element is `size` bytes long, and the `compare` function returns an `int` which is less than, equal to, or greater than zero as the first element it is passed is less than, equal to, or greater than the second. Note that this comparator behavior is the same as that of `qsort()`, thus making life easier for everyone.

14.6 Integer Arithmetic

Two new division functions have been added: `div(int x, int y)` (for `int` division) and `ldiv(long x, long y)` (for `long` division). They return structures (not pointers to structures) of type `div_t` and `ldiv_t` respectively. These structures contain two fields, `quot` and `rem`, which are the quotient and the remainder of dividing the first value by the second.

These functions are primarily useful for two reasons. First, they provide both quotient and remainder in one operation, which can be very efficiently modeled on many machines (especially as a builtin). Second, they provide a well-defined semantic for signed division, which the `/` and `%` operators eschew for purposes of efficiency. For example, given

```
quotient = -8 / 5;
remainder = -8 % 5;
```

there are two possible (`quotient`, `remainder`) pairs: (-1,-3) and (-2,2). The `/` and `%` operators can choose either, while `div()` and `ldiv()` always choose the quotient with the smallest absolute value; that is, they would choose (-1,-3). These semantics are the same as those for FORTRAN division.

14.7 Multibyte Characters and Strings

All the multibyte functions are new. They are `mblen()`, `mbtowc()`, `wctomb()`, `mbstowcs()`, and `wcstombs()` where `wcs` stands for "wide character string", and `mbs` stands for "multibyte string". This area is very implementation dependent, and very little can be said about it intelligently. Although that hasn't stopped me before, in this case I will let discretion win out. If you need to know more, the manual pages on your system will tell you more than I could.

There are likely to be more of these in the future as suggestions are made by those who live with character sets that require wide characters.

14.8 Reserved Identifiers

Identifiers starting with `str` followed by a lowercase letter may appear in this file at a later date. I would not, however, recommend continuously checking this file for such arrivals as a form of entertainment.

Chapter 15 <stdarg.h>

The **<stdarg.h>** mechanism is a replacement for the **<varargs.h>** mechanism, and works almost identically. In fact, it uses the same names for almost everything, unfortunately making it impossible to mix **<varargs.h>** and **<stdargs.h>** in the same file.

<varargs.h> depends on naming the first variable argument something special (namely **va_alist**), whereas **<stdarg.h>** relies on being told the last required argument. **<stdarg.h>** is thus more compatible with the new ellipsis (...) function signature syntax. Here are two examples of its use. The first shows how to use **vfprintf()** (see Section 11.3.1 above); the second loops printing out integers until it reaches the flag value **MAX_INT**.

```
# include       <stdarg.h>

pr_error(
        char    *fmt,
        ...
)
{
        extern int      Line_no;
        extern char     *File_name;
        va_list         argp;

        fprintf(stderr, "%s:%d:", File_name, Line_no);
        va_start(argp, fmt);    /* name the last known argument */
        vfprintf(stderr, fmt, argp);
        va_end(argp);           /* never forget va_end() */
}
```

```
pr_ints(
        int     firstint,
        ...
)
{
        int     curint;
        va_list argp;

        va_start(argp, firstint);
        curint = firstint;
        while (curint != MAX_INT) {
                printf("%d\n", curint);
                curint = va_arg(argp, int);
        }
        va_end(argp);               /* never forget va_end() */
}
```

The second example deserves some comment. One practical difference stemming from the fact that `<stdarg.h>` uses the last named parameter is that there must be at least one named parameter, which was not true with `<varargs.h>`. This means that for a routine (such as our `pr_ints()`) that really takes a terminated list and no *truly* fixed arguments, the first member of the list must be treated specially by having a name, even though it is logically and algorithmically the same as all the unnamed parameters. Our `pr_ints()` routine shows probably the simplest way of handling this, but it does require the creation of a mechanism you might not otherwise have wanted (you wouldn't need `firstint` with `<varargs.h>`).

By the bye, it is tempting to use `va_arg()` directly for expressions that take more than one parameter from the stack:

```
printf(va_arg(argp, char *), va_arg(argp, int));
        /* or */
diff = va_arg(argp, int) - va_arg(argp, int);
```

Because the order of evaluation is not defined within an expression, you cannot be guaranteed which parameter will be fetched from the stack first. In other words, in our `printf()` we might pull the `int` off the stack before the `char *` format. Although the order of evaluation isn't guaranteed in any expression, code that fetches variable arguments seems somehow to be a common place to forget that.

The type `va_list` is a `typedef` name; all the `va_` routines are macros.

Chapter 16 <assert.h>

ANSI has codified the **assert()** macro behavior. Basically, if you **#include <assert.h>**, you can assert an expected truth in your program by simply saying

```
assert(x >= 0 && x <= MAX_X)
```

or whatever. If the assertion is true, nothing happens. If it is false, **assert()** prints an error message and calls **abort()**. If the source is compiled with the symbol **NDEBUG** defined, all invocations of **assert()** become no-ops, without having their values either evaluated or tested; the definition of **assert()** becomes

```
# define        assert(expr)    ((void) 0)
```

Thus, you can use **assert()** to test for conditions that should "never happen", and then, when you feel confident in your code, remove the tests entirely from your execution overhead, while retaining them in the code for when you discover that you were wrong, which you will.

assert() is always a macro; there is no function equivalent for it. This allows it to print out the actual expression that was violated. For example, a violation of the assertion above might print out something like

```
assertion botched: x >= 0 && x <= MAX_X, "gogin.c", line 56
```

If **assert()** was a function, it couldn't get the text of the test that failed, nor the file and/or line number.

Chapter 17 <time.h>

ANSI preserved `time_t` and `clock_t` as scalar values because of existing practice. However, they did not create new types to deal with large times, nor did they adopt specific types and routines from BSD to deal with finer granularities of time than the one-second ticks which UNIX programmers are familiar.

In fact, they punted the whole question of granularity or any direct interpretation of the values of the time types, since this is far too implementation dependent. Instead, routines were provided for dealing with the common manipulations of time.

All the time routines eventually come back to some way of getting a `time_t` from somewhere. The standard way of doing this is calling the `time()` function:

```
time_t
time(
        time_t  *t
);
```

It returns the current time as a `time_t`, and if `t` is not `NULL`, it copies the return value into the `time_t` at which it points. Given this, you can convert it into a broken-down description in a `struct tm` or into string versions.

17.1 New Functions

```
clock_t
clock()
```

Returns the system's best approximation of the time used by the current process. The constant `CLOCKS_PER_SEC` is the number of ticks in a `clock_t` per second, so the value of `clock() / CLOCKS_PER_SEC` is the number of seconds spent thus far on your program. If there is no available processor time, `clock()` returns `(clock_t) -1`.

```
double
difftime(time_t t1, time_t t2)
```

Returns the difference of the two times in seconds. (Note that it returns a **double**, not a **time_t**.)

```
struct tm *
localtime(time_t *t)
struct tm *
gmtime(time_t *t)
```

Each of these takes a time and returns a **struct tm *** which is the time in **t** broken down into its (standard Western) subcomponent parts. These routines are not new, but two things about the breakdown are. First, if the adjustment to Greenwich mean time (GMT) is not known on the system, **gmtime()** is allowed to return **NULL**. Such systems have no concept of "time zone" (which is indeed not universal), and so ANSI dropped all reliance on time zones everywhere. Second, on systems in which the concept of daylight saving time is meaningless (many countries don't have this idea), the **tm_isdst** field of the returned **struct tm** will be a negative number.

```
char *
asctime(struct tm *tp)
```

Some programmers may not be familiar with this function. It turns a broken-down time into a string. It is basically a variant of **ctime()** that takes a pre-broken-down time (**ctime()** takes a **time_t ***).

```
time_t
mktime(struct tm *tp)
```

This new function completes the set of time routines. It takes a **struct tm *** and returns the corresponding **time_t**. It's about time something like this existed. The only thing now missing is something that converts a string form of a date into a **struct tm *** and/or **time_t**. Maybe next time.

```
char *
strftime(char *buf, size_t bufsize,
        const char *fmt, const struct tm *tp)
```

This is a more general form of converting times to strings that takes into account the current locale (see Chapter 23) and allows the programmer to specify a formatting string for the relevant data. The output buffer **buf** is filled in using the **format** string and the broken-down time in **timeptr**.

The format string for **strftime()** is similar to a **printf()** format, and gives you a great deal of control. Format strings are copied in as is unless a directive is encountered — all directives start with a **%**. Each prints out the current locale's version of the specified value, or a value in a specific range. As with **printf()**, to get a **%** you type **%%**.

`%a` Abbreviated weekday name.

`%A` Full weekday name.

`%b` Abbreviated month name.

`%B` Full month name.

`%c` Full date and time output (like `ctime()`).

`%d` Day of the month (01–31).

`%H` Hour for a 24-hour clock (00–23).

`%I` Hour for a 12-hour clock (01–12).

`%j` Day of the year (001–366).

`%m` Month number (01–12).

`%M` Minute (00–59).

`%p` A.M./P.M. designation.

`%S` Second (00–61).(The range goes up to 61 to handle leap seconds.)

`%U` Week of the year with the first Sunday of the year as the first day of week 1 (00–53).

`%w` Day of the week, where Sunday is 0 (0– 6).

`%W` Week of the year with the first Monday of the year as the first day of week 1 (00–53).

`%x` The date part of `%c`.

`%X` The time part of `%c`.

`%y` Year of the current century (00– 99).

`%Y` Year with the current century (for example, 2002).

`%Z` Time zone name, or nothing if the time zone is unavailable or meaningless in this locale.

It is to be freely confessed that the mnemonic value of many of the abbreviations is quite questionable. Why `%a` means "weekday name" or `%I` means "12-hour clock hour" is beyond me. The ANSI committee also seem to use upper- and lowercase distinctions some times and not others (for example, `%H` and `%I` could have been `%h` and `%H` or some such pair). Please complain freely, since it won't do any good.

Using this mechanism it is possible to get exactly the data you want in a locally presentable format. For example, to have your application keep a clock up-to-date, you could simply say

```
/* set time locale to the current locality */
setlocale(LC_TIME, "");

/* ... */

char    Time_fmt = "%X";

update_time()
{
        time_t          t;
        struct tm       *tptr;
        char            clock[100];

        t = time(NULL);
        tptr = localtime(&t);
        strftime(clock, sizeof clock, Time_fmt, tptr);
        display_string(clock);
}
```

Adding a 24-hour-clock option would be as simple as adding a mechanism to change `Time_fmt` to `"10/30/91%H%M%S"`. In fact, you could spend aeons adding a plethora of options that modified `Time_fmt` to do all sorts of things, such as including the date, or having the day appear (in either abbreviated or unabbreviated form), and so on. If you kept this up, you'd have the spiffiest little time display window for your application anyone has ever seen. You would also have no friends. You will have to decide which is more important.

Chapter 18 <errno.h>

This header declares an external **int** called **errno**, which is set by math handling and other routines. It also defines the known error codes it can take on the given system, all starting with the letter **E**.

The only error codes ANSI requires from **<errno.h>**, however, are **EDOM** and **ERANGE**, which are used by the math library (see Chapter 21). You use **errno** as you would under standard UNIX; if a routine that uses **errno** fails, it will make **errno** contain a nonzero value that can be used with **perror()** or **strerror()** (see Section 13.3 above) to describe the type of failure to the user.

Testing **errno** without first having an error flagged by a routine gets you undefined behavior, as it always did.

The committee seriously considered throwing out **errno**, because it can be hard to use, and, because it is set as a side effect, it is very unobvious. For example, if you were using **errno** to detect errors in the math library, it would be hard to figure out which function call in the following code caused the error:

```
errno = 0;

val = sin(angle1) * cos(angle2);
if (errno != 0)
        printf("%s (not sure which angle)\n", strerror(errno));
```

In general, handling errors with **errno** is a pain, but I cannot see what else the committee could have done within their strictures of preserving existing code and avoiding invention of new mechanisms.

18.1 Reserved Identifiers

The ANSI committee had to reserve all macros starting with an uppercase `E` followed by an uppercase letter or digit for future use, even though this grabs a huge chunk of the identifier name space. The convention of naming error codes `ENOSPACE`, `ENOACCESS`, `ENOICE`, and the like is too well established.

Chapter 19 <signal.h>

The header file `<signal.h>` defines a new type `sig_atomic_t` which is an integral type that can be accessed as an atomic entity even in signal handlers. It also must define at least the following signals:

`SIGABRT`
: Abnormal termination (`abort()` uses this).

`SIGFPE`
: A bad arithmetic operation, such as a divide by zero or an over- or underflow (not just floating-point errors, as `FPE` might imply).

`SIGILL`
: An invalid instruction or other bizarreness in the instruction space.

`SIGINT`
: An interactive interrupt, such as control-C.

`SIGSEGV`
: An invalid storage access.

`SIGTERM`
: A termination request ("Please go away cleanly or I'll kill you").

An environment is not required to send these signals, only to allow you to set up handlers for them (thus making such handlers and their setup portable).

However, the new `raise()` call must be allowed to raise these exceptions. For you UNIX geeks, `raise(sig)` is equivalent to `kill(getpid(), sig)`. The `kill()` call is too UNIX specific for ANSI. After all, what is a process ID? What is a process?

If the signal was generated by a `raise()` or `abort()` call, the signal handler may call any library function, and may terminate by returning or by calling `abort()`, `exit()` or `longjmp()`.

However, if the signal came about any other way, a signal handler can call no library function except `signal()` safely within a signal handler, including `longjmp()` or (sigh) output functions like `printf()`. Nor can they reliably access any static data that is not of type `sig_atomic_t`. These things may work on many systems, but code that assumes that they will work is not maximally portable. This restriction is not new. Some existing systems can't handle arbitrary calls inside a signal handler; ANSI is just not requiring everyone to fix this.

As an example of how you would use `sig_atomic_t`, here is a handler for `SIGINT` which, if the program is being run interactively, asks users if they really want to quit:

```
void
interrupt(
        int     sig
)
{
        extern sig_atomic_t     interactive;

        if (interactive && ask("Really quit?") == NO)
                return;
        exit(1);
}
```

If `interactive` was of a type larger than `sig_atomic_t`, and the program was in the middle of setting it when the signal arrived, the value might only be partially updated, and thus it would be unreliable.

Beyond the standard `signal()` parameters `SIG_IGN` and `SIG_DFL`, ANSI has codified a return value of `SIG_ERR` to indicate an error-condition return from `signal()`.

ANSI did not choose between the System V behavior of resetting the signal handler to `SIG_DFL` and the BSD behavior of setting it to `SIG_IGN` when a handler is called.

The first and only guaranteed parameter to the signal handler is an `int`, which is the signal that was raised. Any following parameters, which some systems provide, are non-standard.

19.1 Reserved Identifiers

By now the refrain will be familiar: ANSI has reserved identifiers beginning with `SIG` followed by an upper-case letter or an underscore for future use.

Chapter 20 <setjmp.h>

The **setjmp()** mechanism for nonlocal gotos has been codified without change. After a return from **setjmp()** that was caused by a **longjmp()**, only those local variables declared **volatile** are guaranteed to retain their pre-**longjmp()** values. With all other local variables, you place your bets and you take your chances.

Let us examine the following code, trivial to the point of being useful only as an example:

```
# include       <setjmp.h>
# include       <stdlib.h>

trivial()
{
        jmp_buf         place;
        volatile int    v;
        int             i;

        i = v = 0;
        if (setjmp(place) != 0) {
                /* setjmp() after longjmp() */
                printf("v = %d, i = %d\n", v, i);
                return;
        }
        while (i < 10) {
                v = ++i;
                if (rand() % 10 == 0)
                        longjmp(place, 1);
        }
}
```

We call `setjmp()` to set up the place to which a `longjmp()` will go (remember, `setjmp()` returns zero when it is called for setup). Then we run through a loop ten times, assigning the loop iterator to our `volatile` integer `v`, with a 10% chance of breaking out of the loop each time. If we do break out, we print out the values of `v` and `i` and then return.

Although you expect that `i` and `v` will always have the same value, they may not when you reach the `printf()` after doing a `longjmp()`. This is because the compiler doesn't know `setjmp()` from any other call, and so assumes a normal flow of control, optimizing references to `i` if it wants to. As far as the compiler knows it just set `i` to zero before the first `if` statement. Therefore, it might assume that `i` is zero *inside* that `if` statement. This would allow it to pass the constant `0` to `printf()` (after all, that's the only possible value it can see for `i`). After a `longjmp()` this optimizing assumption will be false. Since `v` is `volatile`, the compiler won't make such assumptions and will always get its current value, and so it will always be correct.

If this all seems a little murky to you, the main point to remember is that if you want to rely on the value of a local variable after arriving at a `setjmp()` from a `longjmp()`, you had better declare it `volatile`.

`setjmp()` is always a macro.

Chapter 21 <math.h>

The header `<math.h>` already exists on most C implementations. In ANSI, it only defines prototypes for floating-point math functions. ANSI did not change the set of math functions; it only (on occasion) tightened up definitions. If you are a numerical analyst, you will care about these, but it is very difficult to give them to you because the entire problem was that each locality defined the semantics according to the native machine operation and the other local languages (such as FORTRAN) that had similar functions, often with highly constrained semantics. This meant that in the areas where numerical people most cared about behavior, existing C compilers had wide variance.

For the most part, ANSI chose to adopt FORTRAN semantics, partly because they are widespread and well known in the numerical community, and partly because this choice allows C compiler implementors to leverage existing FORTRAN implementations.

The macro `HUGE_VAL` remains the standard error code or flag value for many functions. It is, in a sense, like `NULL` — you may not rely on its value, but you can rely on its name. On some machines, it may represent a pattern for ∞.

There are three major types of errors in the math library: domain errors, range errors, and all the others. Domain errors (which are input values out of range) cause an implementation-defined return value, setting `errno` to `EDOM`. Range errors (which are output values out of range) set `errno` to `ERANGE` and return an appropriately signed `HUGE_VAL` on overflow (except `tan()`, which is not required to get the sign right). An underflow returns zero, and may or may not be considered a range error; that's up to the implementation. Math routines are not allowed to signal errors by raising exceptions.

21.1 Reserved Identifiers

For all `double` functions, adding an `f` or an `l` to the function name may invoke a `float` or `long double` version, respectively. Implementations are not required to provide these, but the names are reserved in case someone wants to do so.

Chapter 22 <limits.h> and <float.h>

These new header files define a host of values giving range parameters for integral and system limits (`<limits.h>`) and floating-point values (`<float.h>`). The values of `<float.h>` are of interest to you heavy numerical types, who by now must be used to getting short shrift. I won't bother to write them out here, since most of our readers will not be interested in, say, the number of digits of the radix's base in the significand. There should be a manual page on your system for this header that explains its contents.

For `<limits.h>`, the macros, the minimum values ANSI allows a system to provide (i.e., the minimum maximums), and their meanings are:

Macro	Minimum	Meaning
`CHAR_BIT`	8	number of bits in `char`
`SCHAR_MIN`	-127	min value for `signed char`
`SCHAR_MAX`	+127	max value for `signed char`
`UCHAR_MAX`	255	max value for `unsigned char`
`CHAR_MIN`	(see Note)	min value for `char`
`CHAR_MAX`	(see Note)	max value for `char`
`MB_LEN_MAX`	1	max bytes in multibyte characters
`SHRT_MIN`	-32767	min value for `short`
`SHRT_MAX`	+32767	max value for `short`
`USHRT_MAX`	65535	max value for `unsigned short`
`INT_MIN`	-32767	min value for `int`
`INT_MAX`	+32767	max value for `int`
`UINT_MAX`	65535	max value for `unsigned int`
`LONG_MIN`	-2147483647	min value for `long`
`LONG_MAX`	+2147483647	max value for `long`
`ULONG_MAX`	4294967295	max value for `unsigned long`

Note: If a **char** is **signed** by default in the current implementation, **CHAR_MIN** and **CHAR_MAX** will be the same as **SCHAR_MIN** and **SCHAR_MAX**. If it is **unsigned**, **CHAR_MIN** and **CHAR_MAX** will be 0 and **UCHAR_MAX**, respectively. This, by the way, gives you a handy way to have a **#if** that checks if the default **char** is **signed** or **unsigned** on a given machine.

```
#if CHAR_MIN == 0
        printf("chars are unsigned\n");
#else
        printf("chars are signed\n");
#endif
```

Chapter 23 <locale.h>

There are thousands of assumptions (well, actually thirty-seven) in the C library about how times and dates are interpreted and displayed, how strings are ordered, how numbers are printed, and how currency values are displayed.[1] ANSI had to adapt to the fact that other cultures do these things differently, and they had to do so without breaking existing code. They invented a concept of *locale*, which is a description of how to handle these problems. They have defined a new type, **`struct lconv`**, and two new functions, **`setlocale()`** and **`localeconv()`**. I'm afraid I must refer you to your manual for the full details of **`struct lconv`**, since its actual internals are something most programmers can avoid.

Basically **`setlocale()`** is used to set (or get) the locale-specific type. Before any user code is executed, it is as if the invocation

```
setlocale(LC_ALL, "C");
```

is made. This sets up the defaults with which we are all familiar. The program can make calls to **`setlocale()`** to modify all or part of the locale setting. If the call is successful, or if the string parameter is **`NULL`**, it returns a pointer to a string for the given category. On an error, it returns **`NULL`**. The first parameter can be one of:

`LC_ALL`
: All categories of settings.

`LC_COLLATE`
: String ordering. This affects how **`strcoll()`** and **`strxfrm()`** operate (see Section 13.2 above).

`LC_CTYPE`
: Character set queries of **`<ctype.h>`**.

[1]Well, actually there *are* no C library functions that deal with currencies, but if there were, they would be rife with assumptions. Trust me.

LC_MONETARY
: Monetary formatting codes. There are no defined routines to use this, but there surely will be someday.

LC_NUMERIC
: Numeric formatting characteristics. These are used by the formatted I/O routines, such as `printf()` and `scanf()`, and by the string conversion functions such as `strtod()`.

LC_TIME
: Time formatting. This affects `strftime()` (see Section 17.1 above) and thus `ctime()` and `asctime()`.

A value of `"C"` sets the standard UNIX U.S.-oriented defaults and is called (not surprisingly) the "C locale". A value of `""` sets locale values to those of the implementation-defined "native" environment, whatever that may be. Other strings are interpreted in an implementation-defined way.

A call to `localeconv()` will return a pointer to the current `struct lconv` data. Writing into this structure is not allowed, and future calls to `setlocale()` or `localeconv()` may or may not modify values in the structure pointed at. In other words, `localeconv()` is allowed to return a pointer to its internal static description, and you had better not touch it, because you don't know where it's been. And you'd better cache it if you want to remember it later, since you don't know where it's going.

Surprisingly, there is no variant of `setlocale()` that allows you to pass in a filled-in `lconv` structure; you can only set them by symbolic name.

23.1 Reserved Identifiers

The committee has reserved for future use all names starting with blah, blah, blah ... (Sorry. I just got tired of it. Please excuse me.) What I meant to say was that all macros starting with `LC_` followed by an upper-case letter are reserved for future use by the committee. (The fact that my editor has piano wire stretched around my throat, and threatens to yank unless I take this more seriously, is completely irrelevant.)

Chapter 24 Reserved Identifiers

You've seen scattered through the library descriptions statements about reserved identifiers. Of course, the identifiers defined for the library are reserved. Also, you should not use most identifiers starting with an underscore in a maximally portable program. ANSI has also reserved identifiers starting with certain sequences to allow for future expansion. We present these here all together. Just because we put them under their associated header files doesn't mean that you can use them if you don't include the header; in fact, they are reserved anyway. Read 'em and weep.

`<stdio.h>`
: `%` followed by a lowercase letter in a `printf()` or `scanf()` format string. Use `%%` if you want to be sure to get a `%`.

`<ctype.h>`
: Function names beginning with `is` or `to` and a lowercase letter.

`<string.h>`
: Function names beginning with `str`, `mem`, or `wcs` and a lowercase letter.

`<stdlib.h>`
: Function names beginning with `str` and a lowercase letter.

`<errno.h>`
: Macros beginning with `E` and an uppercase letter (this is the biggest name-space grab).

`<signal.h>`
: Macros beginning with `SIG` or `SIG_` and an uppercase letter.

`<math.h>`
: The names of all existing math functions with a trailing `f` or `l` added (for `float` and `long double` versions, respectively).

<locale.h>

Macros beginning with LC_ and an uppercase letter.

Appendix A Quiet Changes

This appendix lists the "quiet changes" of the ANSI C standard, that is, the changes that will not be flagged as errors or warnings by compilers. If you read nothing else in this book, read this. Then read the rest of the book anyway; it will build character.

Language Changes

(1) Programs that rely (usually accidentally) on internal identifiers being checked only for the first, say, seven characters may get surprised because each distinct spelling will be treated as a separate entity. (Section 2.1)

(2) Integer constants without a type suffix are treated slightly differently. In K&R, decimal constants larger than a signed `int`, and hex or octal constants larger than an **`unsigned int`**, were made `long`; in ANSI decimal constants are as big as they need to be to hold the value, and octal and hex constants with the high bit set are of **`unsigned`** type. (Section 3.3.2)

(3) A compiler may or may not put identical string constants in a single copy in memory. If your program relies on either behavior, it may break. (Section 3.3.3)

(4) Strings that contain `\a`, `\v`, or `\x` may now have different meaning. (Section 3.5)

(5) Because `8` and `9` are no longer valid parts of octal constants, the meaning of `\18` is now equivalent to the character `\1` followed by `8`, not whatever the compiler used to do with an octal 18. (Section 3.5)

(6) Programs with a trigraph sequence in a string (such as `??!`) will have them translated to their trigraph equivalents. (Section 3.6)

(7) A program that relies on preprocessor behavior besides `#`*param* for string versions of parameter names or `##` for concatenation will get (possibly silently) broken. (Section 4.2.2)

(8) Some changes to how constant expressions are evaluated in the preprocessor stage may affect `#if` statements designed to test the execution environment in that a cross-compiler's preprocessor is not required to evaluate all constant expressions exactly as the target machine would.

(9) Programmers who rely on function parameters being widened to `int` or `double` will get their heads handed to them on a dirty platter. And deservedly so, I might add. (Section 5.5.4)

(10) An external function declared in one block is not remembered when that block goes out of scope. This means that existing code may revert to default function-typing rules outside a block rather than use a previous block-constrained declaration. (Section 5.7.1)

(11) Programs that rely on the `unsigned` modifier being propagated through arithmetic operators may change behavior. C now preserves value rather than `unsigned`ness. The ANSI standard's rationale states that "this is considered the most serious semantic change made by the Committee to a widespread current practice." (Section 6.3)

(12) Expressions using only `float` can be evaluated without promotion to `double`, resulting in a speed-up but with a possible drop of precision, potentially changing results of some expressions. (Section 6.4)

(13) With old-style assignment operators going away, expressions that used them and only received (at most) warnings before may now silently work differently. (Section 6.7)

(14) Shift operators no longer take any type information from the count operand. (Section 6.10)

(15) ANSI has reaffirmed how initializers with nested objects (such as arrays of structures) are handled when braces are left out. K&R says they are evaluated in a "top-down" way, but some compilers chose to ignore this and use a "bottom-up" form. This will break code on these broken compilers.

(16) `switch` statements no longer truncate `long` expressions to `int`. (Section 7.1)

Library Changes

Because library implementations vary more widely, this list cannot be exhaustive. In fact, ANSI hardly even tried to touch the subject. I've tried to hit most of the major potential problems.

(1) The `fopen()` append-mode specifier `a` now guarantees that *all* writes will put data at the end of the file, not at the current position. If you've been using this mode for

its "create it only if it doesn't exist" properties, your program will silently fail. This change will most likely affect Version 7 descendent systems, such as BSD. This may be the most deadly quiet change on the library side. (Section 11.2)

(2) File positioning is meaningless after an `ungetc()` call until the ungotten character is read. Some existing systems define position; programs that rely on this will break. (Section 11.4)

(3) An implementation may limit the number of characters that may be pushed back with `ungetc()` to one. If you rely on more, your program may break. (Section 11.4)

(4) `memcpy()` is not required to handle overlapping memory correctly. If your program relies on the fact that it does so on some implementations, it will fail; use `memmove()` instead. (Section 13.1)

(5) When asked to allocate zero bytes, the allocation routines `malloc()` , `calloc()` , and `realloc()` may return either a valid pointer or `NULL` . You may not rely on either behavior, so don't. (Section 14.2)

(6) Programs that rely on any given granularity of `time_t` (the return value from `time()`) are not portable. Also, programs that subtract one `time_t` from another using any method other than `difftime()` are not portable. These are common traps to fall into on UNIX systems, where for quite a while `time_t` has been a `long` with one-second granularity. (Chapter 17)

(7) Programs that rely on `gmtime()` giving a reasonable value, or on the time zone parts of the `struct tm` being returned by `localtime()`, will fail, possibly rudely, on systems where time zone is unknown or meaningless. Also, the daylight saving time field `tm_isdst` may now be negative, meaning there is no such thing as daylight saving time in this area. (Chapter 17)

(8) If you've written library routines that rely on the output of `ctime()`, `asctime()`, or numeric values in `printf()`, or that rely on recognizing numeric formats in `scanf()`, you may be in trouble. Programs that call your routines may use `setlocale()` to change these behaviors. The most common assumption that will break is that the size of the string returned by the `ctime()` and `asctime()` routines is fixed at 25 bytes. When working around these problems, remember to make sure that your routines leave the locale the way they found it. (Chapter 17)

(9) Programs that rely on either the original UNIX behavior or the BSD behavior (which is also the POSIX behavior) for whether signals are blocked or reset to `SIG_DFL` on entry to a signal handler will not be portable, because ANSI allows either semantic. (Chapter 19)

Appendix B Compilation Limits

ANSI guarantees the following minimum maximums for a compilation environment:

8 nesting levels for `#includes`.

8 nesting levels for `#if` forms (`#if`, `#ifndef`, `#ifdef`, and `#elif`).

15 nested levels of compound statements.

12 modifiers of `()`, `[]`, or `*` in a declaration.

31 nesting levels of parenthesized declarators within a full declaration.

32 nested levels of parentheses in an expression.

31 significant characters in an internal identifier or macro name.

6 significant characters in external identifiers, ignoring case.

511 external identifiers in one source file.

127 local identifiers in a block.

1024 macros simultaneously defined in one source file.

31 parameters to a function or macro.

509 characters in a single logical source line.

509 characters in a character string literal (after concatenation).

32767 bytes in a data object.

257 `case` statements for a single `switch`.

127 members of a single `struct`, `union`, or `enum`.

15 nested levels of `struct` or `union` definition.

Appendix C Which Header Is It In?

It can be hard sometimes to figure out which header file you need to include to get a definition of a particular type, variable, function prototype, macro or constant. This appendix gives a list of what is defined where. Some headers require definitions that are also provided by other headers, so you can get some definitions by including one of several files. For example, `<stdio.h>` needs the constant `NULL` so it defines it. If you're not using the standard I/O functions but still want `NULL`, you can include `<stddef.h>` or any other header file it is defined in. Systems are required to make it possible to `#include` more than one file with a given definition. For example, it must be legal to include both `<stdio.h>` and `<stddef.h>` in the same source even though they both may define `NULL`. (A high-quality implementation would, of course, not even generate any warnings.)

Header	*Type*	*Definition*
stdio.h		BUFSIZ
limits.h		CHAR_BIT
limits.h		CHAR_MAX
limits.h		CHAR_MIN
time.h		CLOCKS_PER_SEC
float.h		DBL_DIG
float.h		DBL_EPSILON
float.h		DBL_MANT_DIG
float.h		DBL_MAX
float.h		DBL_MAX_10_EXP
float.h		DBL_MAX_EXP
float.h		DBL_MIN
float.h		DBL_MIN_10_EXP

Header	*Type*	*Definition*
float.h		DBL_MIN_EXP
errno.h		EDOM
stdio.h		EOF
errno.h		ERANGE
stdlib.h		EXIT_FAILURE
stdlib.h		EXIT_SUCCESS
stdio.h		FILE
stdio.h		FILENAME_MAX
float.h		FLT_DIG
float.h		FLT_EPSILON
float.h		FLT_MANT_DIG
float.h		FLT_MAX
float.h		FLT_MAX_10_EXP
float.h		FLT_MAX_EXP
float.h		FLT_MIN
float.h		FLT_MIN_10_EXP
float.h		FLT_MIN_EXP
float.h		FLT_ROUNDS
stdio.h		FOPEN_MAX
math.h	double	HUGE_VAL
limits.h		INT_MAX
limits.h		INT_MIN
locale.h		LC_ALL
locale.h		LC_COLLATE
locale.h		LC_CTYPE
locale.h		LC_MONETARY
locale.h		LC_NUMERIC
locale.h		LC_TIME
float.h		LDBL_DIG
float.h		LDBL_EPSILON
float.h		LDBL_MANT_DIG
float.h		LDBL_MAX
float.h		LDBL_MAX_10_EXP
float.h		LDBL_MAX_EXP
float.h		LDBL_MIN
float.h		LDBL_MIN_10_EXP
float.h		LDBL_MIN_EXP
limits.h		LONG_MAX
limits.h		LONG_MIN
stdio.h		L_tmpnam
stdlib.h		MB_CUR_MAX
limits.h		MB_LEN_MAX

Header	*Type*	*Definition*
assert.h		NDEBUG
locale.h		NULL
stddef.h		NULL
stdio.h		NULL
stdlib.h		NULL
string.h		NULL
time.h		NULL
stdlib.h		RAND_MAX
limits.h		SCHAR_MAX
limits.h		SCHAR_MIN
stdio.h		SEEK_CUR
stdio.h		SEEK_END
stdio.h		SEEK_SET
limits.h		SHRT_MAX
limits.h		SHRT_MIN
signal.h		SIGABRT
signal.h		SIGFPE
signal.h		SIGILL
signal.h		SIGINT
signal.h		SIGSEGV
signal.h		SIGTERM
signal.h		SIG_DFL
signal.h		SIG_ERR
signal.h		SIG_IGN
stdio.h		TMP_MAX
limits.h		UCHAR_MAX
limits.h		UINT_MAX
limits.h		ULONG_MAX
limits.h		USHRT_MAX
stdio.h		_IOFBF
stdio.h		_IOLBF
stdio.h		_IONBF
stdlib.h	void	abort(void)
stdlib.h	int	abs(int i)
math.h	double	acos(double x)
time.h	char *	asctime(const struct tm *tdesc)
math.h	double	asin(double x)
assert.h	void	assert(int expression)
math.h	double	atan(double x)
math.h	double	atan2(double y, double x)
stdlib.h	int	atexit(void (*func)(void))
stdlib.h	double	atof(const char *num)

Header	*Type*	*Definition*
stdlib.h	int	atoi(const char *num)
stdlib.h	long	atol(const char *num)
stdlib.h	void *	bsearch(const void *key, const void *base, size_t num_ele, size_t ele_size, int (*compare)(const void *, const void *))
stdlib.h	void *	calloc(size_t num_ele, size_t ele_size)
math.h	double	ceil(double x)
stdio.h	void	clearerr(FILE *stream)
time.h	clock_t	clock(void)
time.h		clock_t
math.h	double	cos(double x)
math.h	double	cosh(double x)
time.h	char *	ctime(const time_t timeval)
time.h	double	difftime(time_t t1, time_t t2)
stdlib.h	div_t	div(int numerator, int denominator)
stdlib.h		div_t
errno.h	int	errno
stdlib.h	void	exit(int status)
math.h	double	exp(double x)
math.h	double	fabs(double x)
stdio.h	int	fclose(FILE *stream)
stdio.h	int	feof(FILE *stream)
stdio.h	int	ferror(FILE *stream)
stdio.h	int	fflush(FILE *stream)
stdio.h	int	fgetc(FILE *stream)
stdio.h	int	fgetpos(FILE *stream, fpos_t *fpos)
stdio.h	char *	fgets(char *buf, int len, FILE *stream)
math.h	double	floor(double x)
math.h	double	fmod(double x, double y)
stdio.h	FILE *	fopen(const char *file, const char *mode)
stdio.h		fpos_t
stdio.h	int	fprintf(FILE *stream, const char *format, ...)
stdio.h	int	fputc(int ch, FILE *stream)
stdio.h	int	fputs(const char *str, FILE *stream)
stdio.h	size_t	fread(void *buf, size_t ele_size, size_t num_ele, FILE *stream)
stdlib.h	void	free(void *)
stdio.h	FILE *	freopen(const char *file, const char *mode, FILE *stream)
math.h	double	frexp(double x, int *exponent)

Header	*Type*	*Definition*
stdio.h	int	fscanf(FILE *stream, const char *format, ...)
stdio.h	int	fseek(FILE *stream, long offset, int type_flag)
stdio.h	int	fsetpos(FILE *stream, const fpos_t *pos)
stdio.h	long	ftell(FILE *stream)
stdio.h	size_t	fwrite(const void *buf, size_t ele_size, size_t num_ele, FILE *stream)
stdio.h	int	getc(FILE stream)
stdio.h	int	getchar(void)
stdlib.h	char *	getenv(const char *name)
stdio.h	char *	gets(char *str)
time.h	struct tm *	gmtime(const time_t *timeval)
ctype.h	int	isalnum(int ch)
ctype.h	int	isalpha(int ch)
ctype.h	int	iscntrl(int ch)
ctype.h	int	isdigit(int ch)
ctype.h	int	isgraph(int ch)
ctype.h	int	islower(int ch)
ctype.h	int	isprint(int ch)
ctype.h	int	ispunct(int ch)
ctype.h	int	isspace(int ch)
ctype.h	int	isupper(int ch)
ctype.h	int	isxdigit(int ch)
setjmp.h		jmp_buf
math.h	double	ldexp(double x, int exponent)
stdlib.h	ldiv_t	ldiv(long numerator, long denominator)
stdlib.h		ldiv_t
locale.h	struct lconv *	localeconv(void)
time.h	struct tm *	localtime(const time_t *timeval)
math.h	double	log(double x)
math.h	double	log10(double x)
setjmp.h	void	longjmp(jmp_buf env, int retval)
stdlib.h	void *	malloc(size_t size)
stdlib.h	int	mblen(const char *str, size_t len)
stdlib.h	size_t	mbstowcs(wchar_t *wstr, const char *str, size_t len)
stdlib.h	int	mbtowc(wchar_t *wstr, const char *str, size_t len)
string.h	void *	memchr(const void *buf, int value, size_t size)

Header	*Type*	*Definition*
string.h	int	memcmp(const void *buf1, const void *buf2, size_t size)
string.h	void *	memcpy(void *to, const void *from, size_t size)
string.h	void *	memmove(void *to, const void *from, size_t size)
string.h	void *	memset(void *buf, int val, size_t len)
time.h	time_t	mktime(struct tm *tdesc)
math.h	double	modf(double x, double *int_part)
stddef.h	int	offsetof(struct,member)
stdio.h	void	perror(FILE *stream)
math.h	double	pow(double x, double exponent)
stdio.h	int	printf(const char *format, ...)
stddef.h		ptrdiff_t
stdio.h	int	putc(int c, FILE *stream)
stdio.h	int	putchar(int c)
stdio.h	int	puts(const char *str)
stdlib.h	void	qsort(const void *base, size_t num_ele, size_t ele_size, int (*compare)(const void *, const void *))
signal.h	int	raise(int sign)
stdlib.h	int	rand(void)
stdlib.h	void *	realloc(void *buf, size_t size)
stdio.h	int	remove(const char *file)
stdio.h	int	rename(const char *old, const char *new)
stdio.h	void	rewind(FILE *stream)
stdio.h	int	scanf(const char *format, ...)
stdio.h	void	setbuf(FILE *stream, char *buf)
setjmp.h	int	setjmp(jmp_buf env)
locale.h	char *	setlocale(int category, const char *locale)
stdio.h	void	setvbuf(FILE *stream, char *buf, int mode, size_t size)
signal.h		sig_atomic_t
signal.h	void (*)(int)	signal(int sig, void (*func)(int))
math.h	double	sin(double x)
math.h	double	sinh(double x)
stddef.h		size_t
stdio.h		size_t
stdlib.h		size_t
string.h		size_t
time.h		size_t

Header	*Type*	*Definition*
stdio.h	int	sprintf(char *buf, const char *format, ...)
math.h	double	sqrt(double x)
stdlib.h	int	srand(unsigned int seed)
stdio.h	int	sscanf(const char *buf, const char *format, ...)
stdio.h		stderr
stdio.h		stdin
stdio.h		stdout
string.h	char *	strcat(char *to, const char *from)
string.h	char *	strchr(const char *buf, int value, size_t len)
string.h	int	strcmp(const void *str1, const void *str2)
string.h	int	strcoll(const void *str1, const void *str2)
string.h	char *	strcpy(char *to, const char *from)
string.h	size_t	strcspn(const char *str, const char *set)
string.h	char *	strerror(int errnum)
time.h	size_t	strftime(char *buf, size_t size, const char *format, const struct tm *tdesc)
string.h	size_t	strlen(const char *str)
string.h	char *	strncat(char *to, const char *from, size_t len)
string.h	int	strncmp(const void *str1, const void *str2, size_t len)
string.h	char *	strncpy(char *to, const char *from, size_t len)
string.h	char *	strpbrk(const char *buf, const char *set)
string.h	char *	strrchr(const char *buf, int value, size_t len)
string.h	size_t	strspn(const char *str, const char *set)
string.h	char *	strstr(const char *str, const char *substr)
stdlib.h	double	strtod(const char *num, char **end)
string.h	char *	strtok(char *str, const char *set)
stdlib.h	long	strtol(const char *num, char **end, int base)
stdlib.h	unsigned long	strtoul(const char *num, char **end, int base)
locale.h		struct lconv
time.h		struct tm
string.h	size_t	strxfrm(char *to, const char *from, size_t len)
stdlib.h	int	system(const char *command)

Header	*Type*	*Definition*
math.h	double	tan(double x)
math.h	double	tanh(double x)
time.h	time_t	time(time_t *timeval)
time.h		time_t
stdio.h	FILE *	tmpfile(void)
stdio.h	char *	tmpnam(char *buf)
ctype.h	int	tolower(int ch)
ctype.h	int	toupper(int ch)
stdio.h	int	ungetc(int c, FILE *stream)
stdarg.h	*type*	va_arg(va_list argp, *type*)
stdarg.h	void	va_end(va_list argp)
stdarg.h		va_list
stdarg.h	void	va_start(va_list argp, last_param)
stdio.h	int	vfprintf(FILE *stream, const char *format, va_list args)
stdio.h	int	vprintf(const char *format, va_list args)
stdio.h	int	vsprintf(char *str, const char *format, va_list args)
stddef.h		wchar_t
stdlib.h		wchar_t
stdlib.h	size_t	wcstombs(char *str, const wchar_t *wstr, size_t len)
stdlib.h	int	wctomb(char *str, wchar_t wchar)

Appendix D Function Prototypes: Syntax Alternatives

You may have noticed that I'm not too fond of the ANSI prototype syntax. Let me repeat my objections:

(1) There are now two distinct syntaxes for declaring variables in C; the (new) one for function parameters, and the (old) one for everything else.

(2) Parameter declarations are comma separated, instead of semicolon terminated, as other declarations are. This means that you must declare the type of each parameter separately, even if two consecutive ones are of the same type. The prototype

```
double  pow(
                double  x, y
        );
```

will not work, because only `x` is given a type.

(3) The last parameter to a prototype must have the comma left off. This is different from the list in an array or `struct` initialization, in which a trailing comma is optional. Why this is recognized as being useful in one place and not the other is beyond me.

An obvious question is: "What would have been better?" We present two options here; there are probably other ones that would also be superior to the one adopted by the ANSI committee from C++.

D.1 ... (Ellipsis as Forward Reference)

Tom Duff suggested, in a letter published in the July 1984 *SIGPLAN*, another meaning for the ... operator as a forward-reference indicator. He suggested making the prototype syntax just the same as the syntax used in the existing function definition syntax, with ... instead of the function body. For example, the prototype for `strcmp()` would look like this:

```
int
strcmp(s1, s2)
const char      *s1, s2;
{ ... }
```

This use of ... would have several advantages over ANSI's choice, beyond solving the problems mentioned above. First, it is a small, incremental change from the existing C language. Second, the change is intuitive — English speakers, at least, are quite accustomed to using "..." to indicate that something is left out. Lastly, it requires no funky use of `void` to distinguish between an old-style function declaration and a new-style prototype of a function that takes no parameters. The ... form for that would simply be:

```
int
getchar() { ... }
```

D.2 Dropping the Identifier List

The main problem the ellipsis doesn't solve is that you still have to list parameter identifiers in two places: the first as a comma-separated list between the parentheses; the second when you declare their types. (People who let identifiers default to type `int` by not declaring their types should be ashamed of themselves.) To me this seems a small price to pay to avoid the problems of the new syntax. However, if that proved to be the deciding factor to the ANSI committee, I would have suggested eliminating the parameter name list, instead of augmenting it as the ANSI mechanism does. The parameter name list, after all, is the syntactic aberration. Try the following instead:

```
int
strcmp(
        const char      *s1, s2;
);
```

For people who declare parameters in the order they are listed, converting existing functions would then be easy. Given a pre-ANSI function definition:

```
FILE *
fopen(filename, mode)
        const char      *filename, *mode;
{
        /* ... */
}
```

just strip off the name list, and move its closing parenthesis after the type declarations:

```
FILE *
fopen(
        const char      *filename, *mode;
)
{
        /* ... */
}
```

D.3 Invent Your Own

You might be able to think of your own solution. It's Fun! It's Easy! It's Completely Futile! Since ANSI has spoken, there isn't any chance at all that you or I can change this. If you want to play along, here are the rules you must follow:

(1) It must be syntactically different from the existing declarations so that a compiler can determine whether it is looking at old-style function declarations or new-style prototypes.

(2) It must have some way to deal with prototypes for functions with no parameters.

(3) It should be a natural extension to the C language.

Notice that ANSI barely followed that last stricture.

Index